Using Primary Sources

in the Social Studies and Language Arts Classrooms

By
Schyrlet Cameron, Janie Doss, & Suzanne Myers

COPYRIGHT © 2006 Mark Twain Media, Inc.

ISBN 1-58037-388-7

Printing No. CD-404056

Mark Twain Media, Inc., Publishers
Distributed by Carson-Dellosa Publishing Company, Inc.

Table of Contents

Table of Contents (cont.)

About the Book

This book uses primary sources to provide middle school students with an authentic glimpse of history. Designed by educators, this easy-to-follow format helps busy teachers take the work out of using primary sources. The built-in flexibility allows the teacher to start with a historical event, primary document, or children's book and expand in any direction. Each of the historical events contains activities for a lesson, or the lessons can be combined to create a unit. Activities can be adapted to meet the skill level of the students, allowing the teacher to create a positive learning experience. Each lesson contains the following sections:

- Literature Connection features a book with a tie-in to the historical events.

- Correlations to national standards are listed using IRA/NCTE Standards for the English Language Arts, the National Standards for History (NSH), and the standards of the National Council for the Social Studies (NCSS).

- Primary Sources provide a firsthand connection to the historical events.

- Activities promote inquiry-based learning, which allows students to understand historical events.

- Bookshelf Resources are a suggested list of print resources to enhance the study of historical events.

- Related Websites provide opportunities to learn more about the historical events.

Using Primary Sources encourages social studies and language arts teachers and school library media specialists to collaborate. By correlating primary sources with popular children's literature, students see the real-life connection between people and historical events. Using the inquiry-based activities and projects presented in this book creates enthusiasm for teaching and learning.

A component of No Child Left Behind (NCLB) is the 'Enhancing Education Through Technology Act of 2001' (NCLB, Part D). Its purpose is to integrate technology into the elementary and secondary curriculum and instruction with the goal of improving student academic achievement (NCLB, Part D, Section 2402). An additional goal of NCLB is for all students to be "technologically literate" (Section 2402, b2A) by the completion of eighth grade.

Using Primary Sources supports the goals and purpose of NCLB by integrating technology into the middle school social studies and language arts curricula. The lessons use online technology to access and examine historical primary documents. In the activities, students put into practice technology literacy skills by utilizing various technological resources. Integrating technology into the study of primary documents and literature strengthens instruction by providing an avenue for meaningful learning and academic achievement.

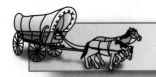
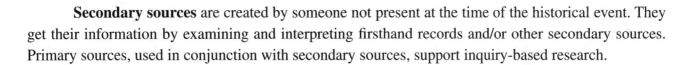

Introduction

What are primary and secondary sources?

A **primary source** is an authentic connection to the past. It is a firsthand record of an event from the perspective of someone present. Primary sources make it possible for students to become voyeurs into the historical event or era.

Some types of primary documents are:

- **Personal Records:** Diaries, journals, letters, manuscripts, autobiographies, memoirs
- **Published Records:** Magazines, newspapers, books
- **Organization or Business Records:** Minutes, reports, correspondence, pamphlets, posters, advertisements, financial ledgers
- **Government Records:** Legislation, court proceedings, deeds, wills, birth and death certificates, marriage licenses, census data
- **Visual Records:** Photographs, paintings, maps, blueprints, video recordings
- **Auditory Records:** Music, oral histories, interviews, speeches
- **Artifacts or Physical Objects:** Clothing, toys, furniture, tools

Secondary sources are created by someone not present at the time of the historical event. They get their information by examining and interpreting firsthand records and/or other secondary sources. Primary sources, used in conjunction with secondary sources, support inquiry-based research.

Why is there a need to evaluate primary sources?

The creation of a primary source record does not mean it is factual or reliable. Students need to understand that whoever created the document had a perspective or bias of the event. For example, if students are reading a firsthand account of the Battle of Gettysburg written by a Union soldier, the student must realize that the account of the battle, while factual, would be biased. This is why it is important that every primary source be evaluated. One method for evaluating the reliability of a primary source is asking the "who, what, why, when, and where" questions.

These questions are:

- Who created the primary source? Does the creator have firsthand knowledge of the event?
- What information is the primary source trying to reveal about the event, or why was it created? Is the purpose to impart information, or is the creator trying to persuade us to his or her perspective or opinion?
- When, in relation to the event, was the primary source created? Was it created at the time of the event, or was it a recalled account as in a memoir?
- Where was the creator when the primary source was created? Was the creator a spectator or participant in the historical event?

Introduction (cont.)

Where can primary sources be located?

Public and private archives and collections provide a wealth of resources for researchers. Within the last decade, there has been a concentrated effort to have primary source collections digitized, making them available via the Internet. Some of the same "who, what, why, when, and where" questions used to evaluate a primary source should be applied to websites providing access to primary sources.

Reprinted primary source materials provide researchers with a diverse selection of primary sources. The middle school library media center should provide access to books that contain collections of speeches and letters. Also, they may provide access to subscription fee databases of primary sources or to microfilm collections. Sometimes, reproductions or transcriptions of primary sources can be found inside a secondary source.

Why should students use primary sources?

National social studies and language arts standards encourage the teaching of historical thinking skills. Using primary sources for inquiry-based learning provides an opportunity for students to develop and practice these skills.

Using primary sources gives students insight into what people thought and felt as events unfolded. Which makes history more real for students, reading the diary entries of Dr. C.S. Taft concerning his care of President Abraham Lincoln immediately after being shot or reading an account of the event in a social studies textbook?

Primary sources provide teachers with unique opportunities to make learning relevant. Teachers should never hesitate to provide opportunities for students to examine and interpret primary sources for historical understanding.

Bibliography

Library, University of California, Berkeley. "Library Research Using Primary Sources." <http://www.lib.berkeley.edu/TeachingLib/Guides/PrimarySources.html>. August 2004.

The Library of Congress. "The Learning Page…: Lesson Overview." <http://lcweb2.loc.gov/learn/lessons/psources/pshome.html>. September 2002.

U.S. National Archives & Records Administration. "Digital Classroom: Document Analysis Worksheets." <http://www.archives.gov/digital_classroom/index.html>. March 2005.

Primary Source Evaluation Worksheet

NAME: _____ DATE: _____

1. Title of the primary source: _____

2. What type of document is the primary source? (choose one)

   ____ newspaper article   ____ journal/diary   ____ map   ____ poster

   ____ political cartoon   ____ photograph   ____ letter   ____ speech

   ____ personal narrative   ____ audio recording   ____ manuscript   ____ artifact

   ____ interview   ____ video recording   ____ other _____

3. Who created the primary source? Does the creator have firsthand knowledge of the event?

   _____

4. What information is the primary source trying to reveal about the event, or why was it created? Is the purpose to impart information, or is the creator trying to persuade us to his or her perspective or opinion?

   _____

   _____

   _____

5. When, in relation to the event, was the primary source created? Was it created at the time of the event, or was it a recalled account as in a memoir?

   _____

   _____

6. Where was the creator when the primary source was created? Was he or she a spectator or participant in the historical event?

   _____

   _____

7. Summarize the information found in the primary source:

   _____

   _____

   _____

   _____

   _____

Jamestown

RELATED THEMES: Colonial Era, Tobacco, Economy, Maps, Propaganda, Persuasive Writing, Fact and Opinion, Compare and Contrast

LITERATURE CONNECTION: Karwoski, Gail. *Surviving Jamestown: The Adventures of Young Sam Collier.* Peachtree. 2001.

Twelve-year-old Sam Collier, an apprentice of Captain John Smith, leaves the hardships of England to sail to the New World. Little does Sam realize that Jamestown Colony has adversity of its own. What he learns in his day-to-day struggles helps him to survive the harsh realities in this New World settlement.

NATIONAL STANDARDS CORRELATION

IRA/NCTE 7: Students conduct research on issues and interests by generating ideas and questions, and by posing problems. They gather, evaluate, and synthesize data from a variety of sources (e.g., print and nonprint texts, artifacts, people) to communicate their discoveries in ways that suit their purpose and audience.

NCSS IIIb: (People, Places, & Environments) create, interpret, use, and distinguish various representations of the earth, such as maps, globes, and photographs

NSH Standard 2G: (Historical Comprehension) Draw upon data in historical maps in order to obtain or clarify information on the geographic setting in which the historical event occurred, its relative and absolute location, the distances and directions involved, the natural and man-made features of the place, the critical relationships in the spatial distributions of those features, and historical events occurring there.

ACTIVITY ONE

Primary Source: http://darkwing.uoregon.edu/~rbear/james1.html
("A Counter-Blaste to Tobacco," Renascence Editions)

Directions: The Jamestown settlers grew tobacco and exported it to England. King James I found the use of tobacco a "vile custome" and addressed this issue in his writing, "A Counter-Blaste to Tobacco." Students examine this article and identify his opinion of smoking. Using the King's reasoning, students develop an advertising campaign that could be used to warn his subjects against the use of tobacco.

ACTIVITY TWO

Primary Source: http://www.virtualjamestown.org/jsmap1.html
("Captain John Smith's Map of Virginia," Virtual Jamestown)

Jamestown (cont.)

Directions: In 1612, John Smith's map of Virginia was published in London. It is an example of the artwork and detail that was used in mapmaking during this time period. Students examine the artistic detail of Smith's map. Using a graphic organizer, they compare and contrast Smith's map to a variety of contemporary maps. Applying the same style and detail exhibited on John Smith's map, students design a map of their community.

Bookshelf Resources

Bruchac, Joseph. *Pocahontas*. Silver Whistle. 2003.

Carbone, Elisa. *Blood on the River: James Town 1607*. Viking. 2006

Edwards, Judith. *Jamestown, John Smith and Pocahontas in American History*. Enslow. 2002.

Fritz, Jean. *The Double Life of Pocahontas*. Putnam. 1983.

McDonald, Megan. *Shadows in the Glasshouse*. Pleasant Company. 2000.

Pierce, Alan. *The Jamestown Colony*. Abdo & Daughters. 2004.

Sewall, Marcia. *James Towne: Struggle for Survival*. Atheneum Books for Young Readers. 2001.

Related Websites

http://www.tobacco.org/History/Jamestown.html
("A Brief History of Jamestown, Virginia," Tobacco.org)

http://www.apva.org/jr.html
("Jamestown Rediscovery," Association for the Preservation of Virginia Antiquities)

http://virtualjamestown.org
("Virtual Jamestown," Crandall Shifflett)

http://www.vahistorical.org/exhibits/tr_james_detail.htm
("Treasures Revealed from the Paul Mellon Library of Americana," Virginia Historical Society)

http://www.socialstudiesforkids.com/articles/ushistory/jamestown.htm
("Jamestown: First English Colony in America," Social Studies for Kids)

http://www.nps.gov/colo/Jthanout/TobaccoHistory.html
("Tobacco: The Early History of a New World Crop," Colonial National Historic Park)

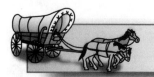

Plymouth Colony

RELATED THEMES: Colonial Era, Mayflower Compact, Pilgrims, Multiple Perspectives, Drama

LITERATURE CONNECTION: Harness, Cheryl. *Three Young Pilgrims.* Bradbury Press. 1992.

Mary, Remember, and Bartholomew Allerton travel from England aboard the *Mayflower* to settle in the New World. This fictionalized account describes the hardships they endured during the voyage and the struggles in their first year in the Plymouth colony.

NATIONAL STANDARDS CORRELATIONS

<u>IRA/NCTE 3</u>: Students apply a wide range of strategies to comprehend, interpret, evaluate, and appreciate texts. They draw on their prior experience, their interactions with other readers and writers, their knowledge of word meaning and of other texts, their word identification strategies, and their understanding of textual features (e.g., sound-letter correspondence, sentence structure, context, graphics).

<u>NCSS IIc</u>: (Time, Continuity, & Change) identify and describe selected historical periods and patterns of change within and across cultures, such as the rise of civilizations, the development of transportation systems, the growth and breakdown of colonial systems, and others

<u>NSH Standard 2E</u>: (Historical Comprehension) Read historical narratives imaginatively, taking into account what the narrative reveals of the humanity of the individuals and groups involved—their probable values, outlook, motives, hopes, fears, strengths, and weaknesses.

ACTIVITY ONE

Primary Source: http://www.historyplace.com/unitedstates/revolution/mayflower.htm
("The Mayflower Compact," The History Place)

Directions: The original Mayflower Compact, which established the first self-government in America, no longer exists. Students examine a handwritten copy of the document recorded in William Bradford's *Of Plimoth Plantation*. They identify the pledges and promises made by the signers of the compact. Working in teams, students create classroom compacts following the format of the Mayflower Compact.

ACTIVITY TWO
Primary Source:
http://content.wisconsinhistory.org/cgi-bin/docviewer.exe?CISOROOT=/aj&CISOPTR=4208
("Bradford's History 'Of Plimoth Plantation'," Wisconsin Historical Society)

Directions: One hundred two *Mayflower* passengers landed in 1620 and immediately began building the first colonial settlement in New England. Students examine William Bradford's account of the passengers' first 30 years in Plymouth and select a passenger to portray. They research the daily life and culture of Plymouth colony. Using their research as a basis for their answers, students, in character, are interviewed in a "live" talk show format.

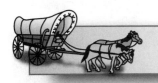

Plymouth Colony (cont.)

ACTIVITY THREE
Primary Source:
http://content.wisconsinhistory.org/cgi-bin/docviewer.exe?CISOROOT=/aj&CISOPTR=4208
("Bradford's History 'Of Plimoth Plantation'," Wisconsin Historical Society)

Directions: In 1620, the *Mayflower* brought 102 settlers to Plymouth Bay. Not everyone aboard the ship was a Pilgrim seeking religious freedom. The majority of passengers were common people hoping to make a better life in the New World. Students examine Bradford's, *Of Plimoth Plantation*. They research the history of the original settlers and daily life in colonial Plymouth. In a living history day presentation, students assume the persona of an original settler going about daily life.

 ## *Bookshelf Resources*

Armentrout, David and Patricia. *The Mayflower Compact*. Rourke Publishing. 2005.

Bradford, William. *Homes in the Wilderness: A Pilgrim's Journal of Plymouth Plantation in 1620*. Shoestring Press. 1988.

Carter, E. J. *Mayflower Compact*. Heinemann Library. 2003.

Fritz, Jean. *Who's That Stepping on Plymouth Rock?*. Coward-McCann & Geoghegan. 1975.

Grace, Catherine O'Neill. *1621: A New Look at Thanksgiving*. National Geographic Society. 2001.

Lasky, Kathryn. *A Journey to the New World: The Diary of Remember Patience Whipple*. Scholastic. 1996.

Mayflower 1620: A New Look at a Pilgrim Voyage. National Geographic Society. 2003.

McGovern, Ann. *If You Sailed on the Mayflower in 1620*. Four Winds Press. 1969.

Poolos, J. *The Mayflower: A Primary Source History of the Pilgrim's Journey to the New World*. Rosen Central Primary Source. 2004.

Rinaldi, Ann. *The Journal of Jasper Jonathan Pierce: A Pilgrim Boy, Plymouth, 1620*. Scholastic. 2000.

Waters, Kate. *Samuel Eaton's Day: A Day in the Life of a Pilgrim Boy*. Scholastic. 1993.

Waters. Kate. *Sarah Morton's Day: A Day in the Life of a Pilgrim Girl*. Scholastic. 1989.

Waters, Kate. *Tapenum's Day: A Wampanoag Indian Boy in Pilgrim Times*. Scholastic. 1996.

Plymouth Colony (cont.)

Related Websites

http://www.mayflowerhistory.com/Passengers/passengers.php
("Complete *Mayflower* Passenger List," MayflowerHistory.com)

http://www.nationalcenter.org/Pilgrims.html
("How the Pilgrims Lived," The National Center for Public Policy Research)

http://www.mayflowerhistory.com/
("Caleb Johnson's Mayflower History.com," MayflowerHistory.com)

http://www.plimoth.org/OLC/index_js2.html
("You are the Historian," Plimoth Plantation, Inc.)

http://teacher.scholastic.com/thanksgiving/mayflower/index.htm
("The First Thanksgiving," Scholastic, Inc.)

http://www.plimoth.org/learn/education/kids/index.asp
("Just for Kids," Plimoth Plantation, Inc.)

Salem Witch Trials

RELATED THEMES: Puritans, Colonial Era, Stereotyping, Trial by Jury, Graphic Organizers, Drama

LITERATURE CONNECTION: Speare, Elizabeth George. *The Witch of Blackbird Pond*. Houghton Mifflin. 1976.

After the death of her grandfather, sixteen-year-old Kit Tyler travels from Barbados to live with her aunt and uncle. The "free spirit" lifestyle enjoyed in Barbados makes it difficult to adjust to life in the narrow-minded and strict Puritan community. Kit secretly develops a friendship with Hannah Tupper, a Quaker widow. When illness hits the community, Hannah and Kit are accused of practicing witchcraft.

NATIONAL STANDARDS CORRELATION

IRA/NCTE 12: Students use spoken, written, and visual language to accomplish their own purposes (e.g., for learning, enjoyment, persuasion, and the exchange of information).

NCSS IId: (Time, Continuity, & Change) identify and use processes important to reconstructing and reinterpreting the past, such as using a variety of sources, providing, validating, and weighing evidence for claims, checking credibility of sources, and searching for causality

NSH Era 2, Standard 2B: The student understands religious diversity in the colonies and how ideas about religious freedom evolved.

ACTIVITY ONE

Primary Source: http://etext.virginia.edu/salem/witchcraft/texts/BoySal1.html ("The Salem Witchcraft Papers, Vol. 1," University of Virginia Library)

Directions: During 1692, many citizens of Salem, Massachusetts, were accused of being witches. These accusations created mass hysteria, leading to numerous court proceedings. Students read through the documents in the case files of Mary Easty. While reading the files, students list the principal characters in her case. Using the case transcripts, students perform a reenactment of the arrest and trial of Mary Easty.

ACTIVITY TWO

Primary Source: http://memory.loc.gov/mss/mcc/003/0001.jpg ("Petition for bail from accused witches, ca. 1692," The Library of Congress American Memory)

Directions: Today, the Bill of Rights guarantees citizens basic civil liberties that were denied to the accused witches at Ipswich Jail. Students read the accused witches' petition for bail. Using a T-chart, they list in the left column the petitioners' reasons for requesting bail. On the corresponding line in the right column, students list the constitutional amendment(s) that would have protected the accused.

FREEDOM OF SPEECH

FREEDOM OF RELIGION

Salem Witch Trials (Cont.)

 Bookshelf Resources

Crewe, Sabrina and Michael V. Uschan. *The Salem Witch Trials*. Gareth Stevens Publishers. 2005.

Fraustino, Lisa Rowe. *I Walk in Dread: The Diary of Deliverance Trembley, Witness to the Salem Witch Trials*. Scholastic. 2004.

Kallen, Stuart. *The Salem Witch Trials*. Lucent Books. 1999.

MacBain, Jenny. *The Salem Witch Trials: A Primary Source History of the Witchcraft Trials in Salem, Massachusetts*. Rosen Central Primary Source. 2003.

Rinaldi, Ann. *A Break with Charity: A Story About the Salem Witch Trials*. Harcourt Brace. 1992.

Uschan, Michael V. *The Salem Witch Trials*. World Almanac Library. 2004.

 Related Websites

http://etext.lib.virginia.edu/salem/witchcraft/
("Salem Witch Trials Documentary Archive and Transcription Project," University of Virginia)

http://school.discovery.com/schooladventures/salemwitchtrials/
("Salem Witch Trials: The World Behind the Hysteria," Discovery.com)

http://www.archives.gov/national-archives-experience/charters/bill_of_rights_transcript.html
("The Bill of Rights," U.S. National Archives & Records Administration)

http://www.law.umkc.edu/faculty/projects/ftrials/salem/salem.htm
("Famous American Trials: Salem Witchcraft Trials 1692," University of Missouri-Kansas City)

http://www.law.umkc.edu/faculty/projects/ftrials/salem/scopesjeopardy%5B1%5D.htm
("Salem Witchcraft Trials Jeopardy," University of Missouri-Kansas City)

Boston Massacre

RELATED THEMES: American Revolution, Trial by Jury, Drama, Multiple Persp... Narrative, Letter Writing

LITERATURE CONNECTION: Rinaldi, Ann. *The Fifth of March*: *A Story of the Boston Ma...* Harcourt. 1993.

Rachel Marsh, a fourteen-year-old girl, is an indentured servant to John and Abigail Adams. It is a time of unrest in the city of Boston. Rachel's loyalty to her master is put to the test when she develops an emotional attachment to a British soldier.

NATIONAL STANDARDS CORRELATION

IRA/NCTE 7: Students conduct research on issues and interests by generating ideas and questions, and by posing problems. They gather, evaluate, and synthesize data from a variety of sources (e.g., print and nonprint texts, artifacts, people) to communicate their discoveries in ways that suit their purpose and audience.

NCSS IIa: (Time, Continuity, & Change) demonstrate an understanding that different scholars may describe the same event or situation in different ways but must provide reasons or evidence for their views

NSH Era 3, Standard 1A: The student understands the causes of the American Revolution.

ACTIVITY ONE

Primary Source: http://www.bostonmassacre.net/trial/acct-adams1.htm
("Speech by John Adams at the Boston Massacre Trial," Boston Massacre Historical Society)

Directions: John Adams defended the four British soldiers accused of inciting the Boston Massacre. Students read Adams' speech that is his argument for the acquittal of the soldiers. Students assume the role of the prosecuting attorney in the case. They examine the depositions, witness testimonies, and the newspaper account found on the related websites. Using their analysis, students write, practice, and present a closing argument.

ACTIVITY TWO

Primary Source: http://www.bostonmassacre.net/gazette/index.htm
("Boston Massacre as reported in the *Boston Gazette*," Boston Massacre Historical Society)

Directions: A detailed account of the Boston Massacre appeared in the *Boston Gazette*. Students read the article to find the point of view. Using the perspective of a Loyalist or Patriot, students write a letter to the editor voicing their reaction to the article.

Boston Massacre (cont.)

Bookshelf Resources

Beier, Anne. *Crispus Attucks: Hero of the Boston Massacre*. Rosen Central Primary Source. 2004.

Draper, Allison, Stark. *The Boston Massacre: Five Colonists Killed by British Soldiers*. PowerKids Press. 2001.

Gillis, Jennifer Blizen. *John Adams*. Heinemann Library. 2005.

Lukes, Bonnie L. *The Boston Massacre*. Lucent Books. 1998.

Mattern, Joanne. *The Cost of Freedom: Crispus Attucks and the Boston Massacre*. Rosen Central Primary Source. 2004.

Ready, Dee. *The Boston Massacre*. Bridgestone Books. 2002.

Santella, Andrew. *The Boston Massacre*. Children's Press. 2004.

Related Websites

http://www.bostonmassacre.net/trial/index.htm
("The Boston Massacre Trial," Boston Massacre Historical Society)

http://www.law.umkc.edu/faculty/projects/ftrials/bostonmassacre/massacrereverelarge.jpg
("*Bloody Massacre*," University of Missouri-Kansas City)

http://www.law.umkc.edu/faculty/projects/ftrials/bostonmassacre/bostonmassacre.html
("Famous American Trials: Boston Massacre Trials 1770," University of Missouri-Kansas City)

http://www.ku.edu/carrie/docs/texts/bostanon.html
("Anonymous Account of the Boston Massacre," AMDOCS. Documents for the Study of American History)

http://douglassarchives.org/hanc_a49.htm
("John Hancock, 'Boston Massacre Oration,' 5 March 1774," Douglass Archives of American Public Address)

http://www.earlyamerica.com/review/winter96/massacre.html
("A Behind-the-Scenes Look at Paul Revere's Most Famous Engraving," Archiving Early America)

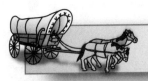

Declaration of Independence

RELATED THEMES: American Revolution, Continental Congress, Workplace Skills, Nonfiction Narrative

LITERATURE CONNECTION: Fritz, Jean. *Will You Sign Here, John Hancock?* Coward-McCann & Geoghegan. 1976.

John Hancock's father died when John was a young boy. He went to live with his uncle, who was a merchant in Boston, Massachusetts. Later, John inherited the business and became one of the wealthiest men in Boston. In 1776, he was the first to sign the Declaration of Independence. He signed his name with great flair, branding himself a rebel and traitor to England and the King.

NATIONAL STANDARDS CORRELATION

IRA/NCTE 5: Students employ a wide range of strategies as they write and use different writing process elements appropriately to communicate with different audiences for a variety of purposes.

NCSS IIe: (Time, Continuity, and Change) develop critical sensitivities such as empathy and skepticism regarding attitudes, values, and behaviors of people in different historical contexts

NSH Era 3, Standard 1A: The student understands the causes of the American Revolution.

ACTIVITY ONE

Primary Source: http://www.archives.gov/national-archives-experience/charters/declaration.html ("Declaration of Independence," U.S. National Archives & Records Administration)

Directions: John Hancock, one of the leaders of the American Revolution and first signer of the Declaration of Independence, had an impressive resumé. He was born in 1737, in Massachusetts, graduated from Harvard College at 17, became a businessman and politician, and was elected president of the Second Continental Congress. Each student prepares a resumé highlighting his or her life achievements. After completing the resumé, each student accesses the primary source website, clicks on the "Join the Signers of the Declaration" icon, and adds his or her signature to a copy of this historical document.

The Resumé of John Hancock

ACTIVITY TWO

Primary Source: http://www.archives.gov/national-archives-experience/charters/declaration.html ("Declaration of Independence," U.S. National Archives & Records Administration)

Declaration of Independence (cont.)

Directions: Fifty-six members of the Continental Congress signed the Declaration of Independence at great personal risks to themselves and their families. King George considered this to be an act of treason. Students select and research one signer of the Declaration of Independence. Applying their research, students compose a one-page biographical sketch. They compile the biographical sketches into a class "Who's Who" book, that includes a table of contents, title page, glossary, index, and cover.

Bookshelf Resources

Burnett, Betty. *The Continental Congress: A Primary Source History of the Formation of America's New Government*. Rosen Central Primary Source. 2004.

Fradin, Dennis B. *The Signers: The Fifty-Six Stories Behind the Declaration of Independence*. Walker & Company. 2002.

Freedman, Russell. *Give Me Liberty!: The Story of the Declaration of Independence*. Holiday House. 2000.

Graves, Kerry A. *The Declaration of Independence: The Story Behind America's Founding Document*. Chelsea. 2004.

Rosen, Daniel. *Independence Now: The American Revolution, 1763-1783*. National Geographic. 2004.

Turner, Ann Warren. *When Mr. Jefferson Came to Philadelphia: What I Learned of Freedom, 1776*. HarperCollins. 2003.

Related Websites

http://www.colonialhall.com/biography.php
("Biographies of the Founding Fathers," Colonial Hall.com)

http://www.usconstitution.net/declarsigndata.html
("Signers of the Declaration of Independence," Steve Mount)

http://www.ushistory.org/declaration/signers/index.htm
("Signers of the Declaration of Independence: Short Biographies on Each of the 56 Declaration Signers," Independence Hall Association)

http://www.historychannel.com/exhibits/declaration/call.html
("The Declaration of Independence: The Call for Independence: How the Declaration Came to Be," A&E Television Networks)

http://www.yale.edu/lawweb/avalon/contcong/07-12-76.htm
("Journals of the Continental Congress: Articles of Confederation and Perpetual Union; July 12, 1776," The Avalon Project)

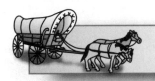
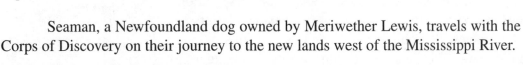

Lewis and Clark Expedition

RELATED THEMES: Corps of Discovery, Louisiana Purchase, Thomas Jefferson, Presidents, Proofreading, Nonfiction Narrative

LITERATURE CONNECTION: Karwoski, Gail Langer. *Seaman: The Dog Who Explored the West with Lewis & Clark*. Peachtree. 1999.

Seaman, a Newfoundland dog owned by Meriwether Lewis, travels with the Corps of Discovery on their journey to the new lands west of the Mississippi River.

NATIONAL STANDARDS CORRELATION

IRA/NCTE 6: Students apply knowledge of language structure, language conventions (e.g., spelling and punctuation), media techniques, figurative language, and genre to create, critique, and discuss print and nonprint texts.

NCSS Ib: (Culture) explain how information and experiences may be interpreted by people from diverse cultural perspectives and frames of reference

NSH Standard 2E: (Historical Comprehension) Read historical narratives imaginatively, taking into account what the narrative reveals of the humanity of the individuals and groups involved—their probable values, outlook, motives, hopes, fears, strengths, and weaknesses.

ACTIVITY ONE

Primary Source: http://memory.loc.gov/cgi-bin/query/r?ammem/mtj:@field(DOCID+@lit(je00048)) ("Thomas Jefferson to Meriwether Lewis, June 1803, Instructions," The Library of Congress American Memory)

Directions: Thomas Jefferson selected Meriwether Lewis to lead the Corps of Discovery. The mission of the expedition would be to explore the best water route for commerce to the Pacific. In addition, they were to develop friendships with the Native American tribes encountered and keep records of the geography, plants, animals, and climate. Students research the Lewis and Clark Expedition. They select a newsworthy event from the mission and write a newspaper article.

ACTIVITY TWO

Primary Source: http://memory.loc.gov/cgi-bin/query/r?ammem/mtj:@field(DOCID+@lit(je00062)) ("Meriwether Lewis to Thomas Jefferson, April 7, 1805, with Invoice," Library of Congress American Memory)

Directions: Incomplete sentences and misspellings are common mistakes in the journal entries of William Clark. In 1805, Meriwether Lewis sent a portion of Clark's private journal back to Thomas Jefferson from Fort Mandan. In his letter, Lewis states, "Capt. Clark does not wish this journal exposed in it's present state, but has no objection, that one or more copies of it be made by some confidential person under your direction, correcting it's grammatical errors &c." Using the April 1, 1805, journal entry by William Clark (see Related Websites), students rewrite the entry using correct grammar, sentence structure, and spelling.

Lewis and Clark Expedition (cont.)

ACTIVITY THREE

Primary Source: http://www.amphilsoc.org/library/guides/lcills.htm
("Lewis and Clark: Illustrations From the Journals," American Philosophical Society Library)

Directions: Some of the members of the Lewis and Clark Expedition recorded their eighteen-month journey for President Thomas Jefferson using journals and field notes. Students examine entries and illustrations from the journals of the Lewis and Clark Expedition. During a walking tour of their community, students journal the plants, animals, people, climate, and geography.

 Bookshelf Resources

Blumberg, Rhoda. *York's Adventures with Lewis and Clark: An African-American's Part in the Great Expedition.* HarperCollins. 2004.

Faber, Harold. *Lewis and Clark: From Ocean to Ocean.* Benchmark Books. 2002.

Myers, Laurie. *Lewis and Clark and Me*: A Dog's Tale. Henry Holt. 2002.

Orr, Tamra. *The Lewis and Clark Expedition: A Primary Source History of the Journey of the Corps of Discovery.* Rosen Central Primary Source. 2004.

Patent, Dorothy Hinshaw. *Animals on the Trail with Lewis and Clark.* Clarion Books. 2002.

Patent, Dorothy Hinshaw. *Plants on the Trail with Lewis and Clark.* Clarion Books. 2003.

Smith, Roland. *The Captain's Dog: My Journey with the Lewis and Clark Tribe.* Harcourt Brace. 1999.

The Lewis and Clark Journals: An American Epic of Discovery: The Abridgment of the Definitive Nebraska Edition. University of Nebraska Press. 2003.

 Related Websites

http://lewisandclarkjournals.unl.edu/
("The Journals of the Lewis and Clark Expedition, edited by Gary Moulton," University of Nebraska Press)

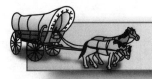

Lewis and Clark Expedition (cont.)

http://ourdocuments.gov/doc.php?doc=17&page=transcript
("Transcript of Jefferson's Secret Message to Congress Regarding the Lewis & Clark Expedition (1803)," The Library of Congress)

http://memory.loc.gov/cgi-bin/query/r?ammem/mtj:@field(DOCID+@lit(je00063))
("Meriwether Lewis to Thomas Jefferson, September 23, 1806," The Library of Congress American Memory)

http://www.lewis-clark.org/
("Discovering Lewis & Clark," VIAs, Inc.)

http://www.nps.gov/jeff/LewisClark2/HomePage/HomePage.htm
("The Lewis and Clark Journey of Discovery," National Park Service)

http://lewisclark.geog.missouri.edu/index.shtml
("Lewis and Clark Across Missouri," University of Missouri)

http://www.mnh2.si.edu/education/lewisandclark/index.html?loc=/education/lewisandclark/home.html
("Lewis & Clark as Naturalists," Smithsonian National Museum of Natural History)

http://www.loc.gov/exhibits/lewisandclark/lewisandclark.html
("Rivers, Edens and Empires: Lewis and Clark and the Revealing of America," The Library of Congress)

http://www.pbs.org/lewisandclark/
("Lewis & Clark," Public Broadcasting Service)

http://nationalgeographic.com/features/97/west/main.html
("Go West Across America With Lewis & Clark!," National Geographic Society)

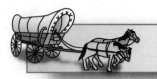

Erie Canal

RELATED THEMES: Transportation, Economy, Graphs, Graphic Organizers

LITERATURE CONNECTION: Harness, Cheryl. *The Amazing Impossible Erie Canal*. Simon & Schuster Books for Young Readers. 1995.

The building of a canal to link Lake Erie to the Hudson River sounded impossible to everyone except De Witt Clinton. After eight years of hard labor, he proved the skeptics wrong.

NATIONAL STANDARDS CORRELATION

<u>IRA/NCTE 12:</u> Students use spoken, written, and visual language to accomplish their own purposes (e.g., for learning, enjoyment, persuasion, and the exchange of information).

<u>NCSS Va:</u> (Individuals, Groups, & Institutions) demonstrate an understanding of concepts such as role, status, and social class in describing the interactions of individuals and social groups

<u>NSH Standard 2H:</u> (Historical Comprehension) Utilize visual, mathematical, and quantitative data presented in charts, tables, pie and bar graphs, flow charts, Venn diagrams, and graphic organizers to clarify, illustrate, or elaborate upon information presented in the historical narrative.

ACTIVITY ONE

Primary Source: http://www.history.rochester.edu/canal/bib/springer/
("*Monthly Labor Review*: Canal Boat Children," University of Rochester)

Directions: Men working on the canal boats were separated from their families on shore for long periods of time. Others chose to take their families with them on the canals. In 1921, three hundred fifty-four children were found living on canal boats. Due to this lifestyle, children endured many harsh living conditions. Using the primary source, students list the hardships faced by canal boat children. Students design posters illustrating the similarities and differences between their lifestyles and that of the canal boat children.

ACTIVITY TWO

Primary Source: http://www.history.rochester.edu/canal/map/1899boat.jpg
("Erie Canal Boats," University of Rochester)

Directions: The Erie Canal provided a waterway for transporting goods between the Great Lakes and the East. When the Erie Canal was completed in 1817, canal boats had the capacity of holding 30 tons of wheat. At the end of the canal era, boats had the capacity of holding 1,000 tons of wheat. Students examine the primary source to discover the changes in the hauling capacity of canal boats from 1817–1899. Students create a graph illustrating these changes.

Erie Canal (cont.)

Bookshelf Resources

Doherty, Craig A. *The Erie Canal*. Blackbirch Press. 1997.

Levy, Janey. *The Erie Canal: A Primary Source History of the Canal That Changed America*. Rosen Central Primary Source. 2003.

Myers, Anna. *Hoggee*. Walker & Company. 2004.

Santella, Andrew. *The Erie Canal*. Compass Point Books. 2005.

Spier, Peter. *The Erie Canal*. Doubleday. 1970.

Stein, R. Conrad. *The Erie Canal*. Children's Press. 2004.

Thompson, Linda. *The Erie Canal*. Rourke. 2005.

Related Websites

http://www.canals.state.ny.us/cculture/history/
("The Erie Canal: A Brief History," New York State Canals)

http://www.eduplace.com/ss/hmss/8/unit/act4.1.2.html
("Low Bridge, Everybody Down (The Erie Canal) by Thomas S. Allen," Houghton Mifflin Company)

http://www.history.rochester.edu/canal/
("Department of History: History of the Erie Canal," New York State Canal System)

http://www.history.rochester.edu/canal/map/1868ny.jpg
("State of New York Showing its Canals and Railroads 1868," New York State Canal System)

http://memory.loc.gov/ammem/ndlpedu/lessons/00/canal/boats.html
("Images from the Book *Marco Paul's Travels on the Erie Canal*," The Library of Congress American Memory)

http://www.eriecanal.org/images.html
("Images of the Erie Canal," Frank E. Sadowski, Jr.)

http://lcweb2.loc.gov/rbc/rbpe/rbpe12/rbpe120/1200020a/001dr.jpg
("Table of the New Rates of Toll on the Erie Canal," The Library of Congress American Memory)

Trail of Tears

RELATED THEMES: Indian Removal Act of 1830, Andrew Jackson, The Cherokee Nation, Presidents, Trails, Stereotyping, Migration, Graphic Organizers, Compare and Contrast, Multiple Perspectives

LITERATURE CONNECTION: Bruchac, Joseph. *The Journal of Jesse Smoke: A Cherokee Boy.* Scholastic. 2001.

In October 1837, Jesse Smoke, a Cherokee, starts his journal to record the events affecting him, his family, and the Cherokee Nation. Over the next sixteen months, he records the forced removal and relocation march of his people on what is known as the "Trail of Tears."

NATIONAL STANDARDS CORRELATION

<u>IRA/NCTE 3</u>: Students apply a wide range of strategies to comprehend, interpret, evaluate, and appreciate texts. They draw on their prior experience, their interactions with other readers and writers, their knowledge of word meaning and of other texts, their word identification strategies, and their understanding of textual features (e.g., sound-letter correspondence, sentence structure, context, graphics).

<u>NCSS IIc</u>: (Time, Continuity, & Change) identify and describe selected historical periods and patterns of change within and across cultures, such as the rise of civilizations, the development of transportation systems, the growth and breakdown of colonial systems, and others

<u>NSH Era 4, Standard 1B:</u> The student understands federal and state Indian policy and the strategies for survival forged by Native Americans.

ACTIVITY ONE
Primary Source:
http://memory.loc.gov/cgi-bin/ampage?collId=llsl&fileName=004/llsl004.db&recNum=458
("Statutes at Large, 21st Congress, 1st Session, Page 411," The Library of Congress American Memory)

Directions: Soon after becoming president, Andrew Jackson asked Congress to pass an act to force the removal of Native Americans off their lands. These lands east of the Mississippi River would be exchanged for unsettled lands west of the river. In 1942, President Franklin D. Roosevelt would force the relocation of the Japanese-Americans with Executive Order 9066 (see Related Websites). Students compare and contrast the two documents using a graphic organizer.

ACTIVITY TWO
Primary Source: http://memory.loc.gov/cgi-bin/query/r?ammem/rbpe:@field(DOCID+@lit(rbpe1740 400a))
("Orders No. 25 Headquarters, Eastern Division. Cherokee Agency, Ten. May 17, 1838," The Library of Congress)

Trail of Tears (cont.)

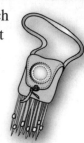

Directions: General Winfield Scott issued orders to the troops who would force march the Native Americans to lands west of the Mississippi. These orders were to be "read at the head of each company." The teacher reads Orders No. 25 to the students. Using a soldier's perspective, students write a personal reflection concerning the orders. Also, General Winfield Scott publicly addressed the Cherokee Nation (see Related Websites). The teacher reads Scott's address to the students. Using a Cherokee's perspective, students write a personal reflection concerning Scott's address.

 ### *Bookshelf Resources*

Bealer, Alex W. *Only the Names Remain: The Cherokees and the Trail of Tears*. Little, Brown. 1996.

Birchfield, D. L. *The Trail of Tears*. World Almanac Library. 2004.

Byers, Ann. *The Trail of Tears: A Primary Source History of the Forced Relocation of the Cherokee Nation*. Rosen Central Primary Source. 2004.

Elish, Dan. *The Trail of Tears: The Story of the Cherokee Removal*. Benchmark Books. 2002.

Salas, Laura Purdie. *The Trail of Tears, 1838*. Bridgestone Books. 2003.

Voices from the Trail of Tears. J. F. Blair. 2003.

 ### *Related Websites*

http://www.ourdocuments.gov/doc.php?doc=74&page=transcript
("Transcript of Executive Order 9066: Japanese Relocation Order (1942)," U.S. National Archives & Records Administration)

http://www.cviog.uga.edu/Projects/gainfo/scottadd.htm
("General Winfield Scott's Address to the Cherokee Nation, May 10, 1838," Carl Vinson Institute of Government)

http://www.cherokee.org/home.aspx?section=culture&culture=history&cat=R
("Trail of Tears Era," The Cherokee Nation)

http://www.ourdocuments.gov/doc.php?flash=true&doc=25
("President Andrew Jackson's Message to Congress 'On Indian Removal' (1830),"
U.S. National Archives & Records Administration)

http://www.nhc.rtp.nc.us/tserve/nattrans/ntecoindian/essays/indianremovalg.htm
("The Effect of Removal on American Indian Tribes," National Humanities Center)

Battle of the Alamo

RELATED THEMES: Texas Independence, Manifest Destiny, Sam Houston, Davy Crockett, Nonfiction Narrative, Public Speaking

LITERATURE CONNECTION: Garland, Sherry. *A Line in the Sand: The Alamo Diary of Lucinda Lawrence, Gonzales, Texas, 1835*. Scholastic. 1998.

Twelve-year-old Lucinda Lawrence chronicles in her journal the events of her life. Lucinda tells of the turmoil facing the people of Texas in 1835, as they are forced to battle for their independence.

NATIONAL STANDARDS CORRELATION

IRA/NCTE 7: Students conduct research on issues and interests by generating ideas and questions and by posing problems. They gather, evaluate, and synthesize data from a variety of sources (e.g., print and nonprint texts, artifacts, people) to communicate their discoveries in ways that suit their purpose and audience.

NCSS IVc: (Individual Development & Identity) describe the ways family, gender, ethnicity, nationality, and institutional affiliations contribute to personal identity

NSH Standard 3B: (Historical Analysis and Interpretation) Consider multiple perspectives of various peoples in the past by demonstrating their differing motives, beliefs, interests, hopes, and fears.

ACTIVITY ONE

Primary Source: http://www.freedomdocuments.com/Travis/enlarge.html
("Letter written from the Siege of the Alamo by Colonel William Barret Travis," Historical Documents Reproduction, Inc.)

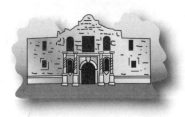

Directions: William Barret Travis, commander at the Alamo, sent out a plea for help to "The People of Texas and all Americans in the world." Help did not arrive in time to save those men who shared his view of "Victory or Death." Many "famous" men were among those who sacrificed their lives for independence. Students research the life history of one of the men who fought at the Battle of the Alamo and write his obituary.

ACTIVITY TWO

Primary Source: http://www.coppiniacademy.com/alamo_heroes_cenotaph.htm
("The Alamo Heroes Cenotaph," The Coppini Academy of Fine Arts)

Directions: The Alamo Heroes Cenotaph is a memorial to all the men who fought and died at the Battle of the Alamo. Each student researches a United States War memorial or monument. Using their research, they design an informational poster to be used as a visual aid in an oral presentation.

Battle of the Alamo (cont.)

 Bookshelf Resources

Edmondson, J. R. *Jim Bowie: Frontier Legend, Alamo Hero*. PowerPlus Books. 2003.

Garland, Sherry. *In the Shadow of the Alamo*. Harcourt. 2001.

Garland, Sherry. *Voices of the Alamo*. Scholastic. 2000.

Levy, Jane. *The Alamo: A Primary Source History of the Legendary Texas Mission*. Rosen Central Primary Source. 2003.

Murphy, Jim. *Inside the Alamo*. Delacorte Press. 2003.

Riehecky, Janet. *The Siege of the Alamo*. World Almanac Library. 2002.

Sorrels, Roy. *The Alamo in American History*. Enslow. 1996.

Tanaka, Shelley. *The Alamo: Surrounded and Outnumbered They Choose to Make a Defiant Last Stand*. Hyperion Books for Children. 2003.

 Related Websites

http://www.thealamo.org/words.html
("The Alamo: In Their Own Words," Daughters of the Republic of Texas)

http://www.lone-star.net/mall/texasinfo/alamo-battle.htm
("The Battle of the Alamo," Lone Star Internet)

http://www.pbs.org/wgbh/amex/alamo/peopleevents/index.html
("Remembering the Alamo," Public Broadcasting Service)

http://americanhistory.about.com/od/monuments/
("United States Monuments," A PRIMEDIA Company)

http://www.abmc.gov/memorials/index.php
("Memorials," American Battle Monuments Commission)

http://www.digitalhistory.uh.edu/learning_history/alamo/alamo_preparations.cfm
("Explorations: Remembering the Alamo," Digital History)

http://www.tsha.utexas.edu/handbook/online/articles/view/CC/fcr24.html
("Crockett, David," The Handbook of Texas Online)

Oregon Trail

RELATED THEMES: Manifest Destiny, Migration, Pioneers, Trails, Maps, Technical Writing

LITERATURE CONNECTION: Spooner, Michael. *Daniel's Walk*. Henry Holt. 2001.

Daniel is told that his long-lost father needs his help. Determined to come to his rescue, Daniel walks from Missouri to Oregon. He encounters trouble with every step of his journey.

NATIONAL STANDARDS CORRELATION

IRA/NCTE 5: Students employ a wide range of strategies as they write and use different writing process elements appropriately to communicate with different audiences for a variety of purposes.

NCSS IIIb: (People, Places, & Environments) create, interpret, use, and distinguish various representations of the earth, such as maps, globes, and photographs

NSH Standard 2G: (Historical Comprehension) Draw upon data in historical maps in order to obtain or clarify information on the geographic setting in which the historical event occurred, its relative and absolute location, the distances and directions involved, the natural and man-made features of the place, and critical relationships in the spatial distributions of those features and historical events occurring there.

ACTIVITY ONE

Primary Source: http://www.lib.utexas.edu/maps/historical/oregontrail_1907.jpg
("Line of Original Emigration to the Pacific Northwest Commonly Known as the Oregon Trail," The University of Texas at Austin)

Directions: Settlers faced many hardships on the way west, especially the terrain. Using the primary source as a guide, students transfer the Oregon Trail route on to a contemporary, physical map of the United States. Students examine the map to identify natural obstacles the pioneers faced. They design an Oregon Trail handbook that would help the pioneers prepare for these obstacles.

ACTIVITY TWO

Primary Source: http://www.lib.utexas.edu/maps/historical/oregontrail_1907.jpg
("Line of Original Emigration to the Pacific Northwest Commonly Known as the Oregon Trail," The University of Texas at Austin)

Directions: The pioneers' trip over the Oregon Trail was not easy. Settlers were faced with many natural obstacles, including rivers, flatlands, deserts, and mountains. Students research the actual topography of the trail. Using salt and flour dough, they create three-dimensional Oregon Trail maps.

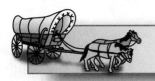

Oregon Trail (cont.)

 ## *Bookshelf Resources*

Blackwood, Gary L. *Life on the Oregon Trail*. Lucent. 1999.

Galford, Ellen. *The Trail West: Exploring History Through Art*. Two-Can Publishing. 2005.

Gregory, Kristiana. *Across the Wide and Lonesome Prairie: The Oregon Trail Diary of Hattie Campbell*. Scholastic. 1997.

Hester, Sallie. *A Covered Wagon Girl: The Diary of Sallie Hester, 1849–1850*. Blue Earth Books. 2000.

Levine, Ellen. *The Journal of Jedekiah Barstow: An Emigrant on the Oregon Trail*. Scholastic. 2002.

Moss, Marissa. *Rachel's Journal: The Story of a Pioneer Girl*. Harcourt Brace. 1998.

Woodruff, Elvira. *Dear Levi: Letters From the Overland Trail*. Knopf. 1994.

 ## *Related Websites*

http://www.multihobbies.com/saltdough/recipes.htm
("Salt Dough, Easy and Quick to Prepare," MultiHobbies.com)

http://www.kancoll.org/books/marcy/macont.htm
("*The Prairie Traveler* by Randolph B. Marcy, Captain, U.S.A.," The Kansas Collection)

http://www.endoftheoregontrail.org/maplibrary/oregontrail.html
("Route of the Oregon Trail," End of the Trail Interpretive Center)

http://www.isu.edu/~trinmich/Oregontrail.html
("The Oregon Trail," Boettcher/Trinklein, Inc.)

http://www.americanwest.com/trails/pages/oretrail.htm
("The Oregon Trail," AmericanWest.com)

http://xroads.virginia.edu/~HYPER/OREGON/oregon.html
("*The Oregon Trail: Sketches of Prairie and Rocky-Mountain Lif*e by Francis Parkman," American Studies at the University of Virginia)

Underground Railroad

RELATED THEMES: Slavery, Abolitionist, Civil War, Harriet Tubman, Missouri Compromise, Compromise of 1850, Stereotyping, Multiple Perspectives, Fictional Narrative

LITERATURE CONNECTION: Wisler, G. Clifton. *Caleb's Choice*. Dutton. 1996.

Caleb's father loses the family's money and possessions in a land speculation deal. Caleb is sent to live with his grandmother, an innkeeper, in Texas. In 1858, people are divided over the Fugitive Slave Law. The law makes it illegal to aid runaway slaves. Caleb has to choose whether or not to break the law by helping two runaway slaves.

NATIONAL STANDARDS CORRELATION

IRA/NCTE 7: Students conduct research on issues and interests by generating ideas and questions and by posing problems. They gather, evaluate, and synthesize data from a variety of sources (e.g., print and nonprint texts, artifacts, people) to communicate their discoveries in ways that suit their purpose and audience.

NCSS Vb: (Individuals, Groups, & Institutions) analyze group and institutional influences on people, events, and elements of culture

NSH Era 4, Standard 4A: The student understands the abolitionist movement.

ACTIVITY ONE

Primary Source:

http://memory.loc.gov/cgi-bin/ampage?collId=llsl&fileName=009/llsl009.db&recNum=489

("*Statutes at Large, 31st Congress, 1st Session,* page 462," The Library of Congress American Memory)

Directions: As territories applied to become states, there was always an argument on whether they would be admitted as free or slave. In 1849, the disagreement came up again when California applied for statehood and the Utah and New Mexico territories were ready to be organized. The issue was resolved with the Compromise of 1850. Contained within the compromise were the Fugitive Slave Laws. Students examine the primary source to determine how these laws affected abolitionists. They research the abolitionist movement, focusing on people, organizations, and events. Using their research, students design fact cards with an illustration on one side and a brief biographical or historical sketch on the other.

Underground Railroad (cont.)

ACTIVITY TWO

Primary Source: http://hdl.loc.gov/loc.rbc/rbpe.08600200
("$200 reward. Ranaway from the subscriber on the night of Thursday, the 30th of September. Five negro slaves ... Wm. Russell. St. Louis, Oct. 1, 1847," The Library of Congress American Memory)

Directions: Many people risked their lives to help runaway slaves escape to "free" territories or states. The network of safe houses and volunteers was known as the Underground Railroad. Slave owners would offer rewards to slave hunters to find and return runaways. Students research the Underground Railroad. After examining the primary source, students create a historical narrative of the escape from the perspective of one of the family members listed on the poster.

ACTIVITY THREE

Primary Source: http://scriptorium.lib.duke.edu/sheetmusic/n/n05/n0570.10/
("Swing Low, Sweet Chariot," Duke University)

Directions: Many Americans became convinced slavery was wrong and joined the Abolitionist Movement. Some were willing to risk their lives to help slaves escape to freedom on the Underground Railroad. Song lyrics with hidden meanings were used to assist slaves in finding safe escape routes. Students examine the primary source for coded messages. Also, oral tradition relates that quilt patterns contained coded messages. Students research the Underground Railroad and design a quilt block using their own symbols to create a coded message. The blocks are combined to make a classroom freedom quilt.

 Bookshelf Resources

Altman, Linda Jacobs. *Slavery and Abolition in American History*. Enslow. 1999.

Edwards, Judith. *Abolitionists and Slave Resistance*. Enslow. 2004.

Hansen, Joyce. *Freedom Roads: Searching for the Underground Railroad*. Cricket Books. 2003.

Haskins, James. *Get on Board: The Story of the Underground Railroad*. Scholastic. 1993.

Hopkinson, Deborah. *Sweet Clara and the Freedom Quilt*. Knopf. 1993.

Underground Railroad (cont.)

Houston, Gloria. *Bright Freedom's Song: A Story of the Underground Railroad*. Harcourt Brace. 1998.

Sawyer, Kem Knapp. *The Underground Railroad in American History*. Enslow. 1997.

Tackach, James. *The Abolition of American Slavery*. Lucent Books. 2002.

Wolny, Philip. *The Underground Railroad: A Primary Source History of the Journey to Freedom*. Rosen Central Primary Source. 2004.

Woodruff, Elvira. *Dear Austin: Letters From the Underground Railroad*. Knopf. 1998.

Related Websites

http://www.vlib.us/amdocs/texts/canadian_slaves.html
("Testimony of the Canadian Fugitive," The University of Kansas)

http://www.cr.nps.gov/aahistory/ugrr/ugrr.htm
("Our Shared History African American Heritage: Underground Railroad," National Park Service)

http://www.library.cornell.edu/mayantislavery/maysearch.htm
("Samuel J. May Anti-Slavery Movement Collection," Cornell University Library)

http://www.loc.gov/exhibits/african/afam006.html
("African-American Mosaic," The Library of Congress)

http://www.loc.gov/exhibits/odyssey/archive/03/0320001r.jpg
("Reynolds's Political Map of the United States," The Library of Congress)

http://education.ucdavis.edu/NEW/STC/lesson/socstud/railroad/SlaveLaw.htm
("The Fugitive Slave Bill of 1850," University of California Davis)

http://www.nationalgeographic.com/railroad/j1.html
("The Underground Railroad," National Geographic Society)

http://www.pbs.org/wgbh/aia/part4/title.html
("Judgement Day," Public Broadcasting Service)

Pony Express

RELATED THEMES: Workplace Skills

LITERATURE CONNECTION: Gregory, Kristiana. *Jimmy Spoon and the Pony Express*. Scholastic. 1994.

Jimmy Spoon saw a newspaper headline advertising for Pony Express riders. Bored with city life, he signed the contract and took the required oath. He became one of the eighty boys hired to carry the mail from St. Joseph, Missouri, to Sacramento, California.

NATIONAL STANDARDS CORRELATION

IRA/NCTE 12: Students use spoken, written, and visual language to accomplish their own purposes (e.g., for learning, enjoyment, persuasion, and the exchange of information).

NCSS IIe: (Time, Continuity, & Change) develop critical sensitivities such as empathy and skepticism regarding attitudes, values, and behaviors of people in different historical contexts

NHS Standard 4B: (Historical Research Capabilities) Obtain historical data from a variety of sources, including: library and museum collections, historic sites, historical photos, journals, diaries, eyewitness accounts, newspapers, and the like; documentary films, oral testimony from living witnesses, censuses, tax records, city directories, statistical compilations, and economic indicators.

ACTIVITY ONE

Primary Source: http://www.nps.gov/poex/hrs/images/fig4.jpg

("Pony Express St. Joseph, Missouri, to California in Ten Days or Less," National Park Service)

Directions: In 1860, advertisements for Pony Express riders started to appear in newspapers all across the West. Hundreds of young boys seeking excitement and adventure applied for the job. Students examine the Pony Express advertisement to identify physical traits and qualifications required for riders. Then students research the history of the Pony Express. Using the research information and requirements for riders, students create a Pony Express job application.

ACTIVITY TWO

Primary Source: http://www.pbs.org/weta/thewest/resources/archives/four/64_02.htm

("Frank E. Webner, Pony Express Rider, ca. 1861," Public Broadcasting Service)

Directions: Many young boys dreamed of becoming a Pony Express rider. They were considered the heroes of their time. Students research the life of one of the Pony Express riders (see Related Websites). Using the information, they create a comic strip emphasizing the hardships riders endured while delivering the mail to California.

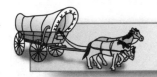

Pony Express (cont.)

 ## *Bookshelf Resources*

Anderson, Peter. *The Pony Express*. Children's Press. 1996.

Dolan, Edward F. *The Pony Express*. Benchmark Books. 2003.

Harness, Cheryl. *They're Off!: The Story of the Pony Express*. Simon & Schuster Books for Young Readers. 1996.

Marcy, Randolph Barnes. *The Prairie Traveler: A Hand-Book for Overland Expeditions, With Maps, Illustrations, and Itineraries of the Principal Routes Between the Mississippi and the Pacific*. Applewood Books. 1993.

Payment, Simone. *The Pony Express: A Primary Source History of the Race to Bring Mail to the American West*. Rosen Central Primary Source. 2005.

Yancey, Diane. *Life of the Pony Express*. Lucent. 2001.

 ## *Related Websites*

http://www.npr.org/programs/wesat/features/2003/aug/ponyexpress/poster.html
("Pony Express," National Park Service)

http://www.ponyexpress.org/museum_history.htm
("About the Pony Express," The Pony Express National Museum)

http://www.americanwest.com/trails/pages/ponyexp1.htm
("Pony Express Information," AmericanWest.com)

http://www.nps.gov/poex/hrs/hrs.htm
("*Pony Express National Historic Trail*: Historic Resource Study," National Park Service)

http://www.schoolhousevideo.org/Media/local-ponyexp-cover2.JPG
("Pony Express stamped envelope," School House Video)

http://www.stjosephmuseum.org/PonyExpress/history.html
("The History," St. Joseph Museums Inc.)

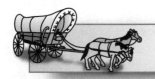

Gettysburg Address

RELATED THEMES: Civil War, Abraham Lincoln, Presidents, Fictional Narrative, Public Speaking, Journaling

LITERATURE CONNECTION: Banks, Sara Harrell. *Abraham's Battle: A Novel of Gettysburg.* Atheneum Books for Young Readers. 1999.

In 1863, the Civil War comes to Gettysburg, Pennsylvania, the home of Abraham Small, a freed slave. Feeling the need to do his share, he becomes an ambulance driver during the Battle of Gettysburg, and witnesses firsthand the reality of war. Weeks later, at the dedication of the cemetery, he hears Abraham Lincoln give his Gettysburg Address.

NATIONAL STANDARDS CORRELATION

<u>IRA/NCTE 4:</u> Students adjust their use of spoken, written, and visual language (e.g., conventions, style, vocabulary) to communicate effectively with a variety of audiences and for different purposes.

<u>NCSS IIe:</u> (Time, Continuity, & Change) develop critical sensitivities such as empathy and skepticism regarding attitudes, values, and behaviors of people in different historical context

<u>NSH Standard 2C:</u> (Historical Comprehension) Identify the central question(s) the historical narrative addresses and the purpose, perspective, or point of view from which it has been constructed.

ACTIVITY ONE

Primary Source: http://www.loc.gov/exhibits/treasures/trt031.html
("An Official Invitation to Gettysburg," The Library of Congress)

Directions: President Abraham Lincoln was invited by Judge David Wills to play a minor role in the dedication ceremony of the Gettysburg Memorial Cemetery. Students examine the letter focusing on its literary form. Using the same style and format, they compose a letter from President Lincoln to Judge David Wills accepting the invitation.

ACTIVITY TWO

Primary Source: http://www.loc.gov/exhibits/gadd/gadrft.html
("The Gettysburg Address Drafts," The Library of Congress)

Directions: On November 19, 1863, President Lincoln delivered his famous, brief speech at the dedication ceremony of the Gettysburg Memorial Cemetery. Students present their own dramatic interpretation of the Gettysburg Address, demonstrating public-speaking skills (e.g., voice level, tone, inflection) necessary to communicate effectively with an audience.

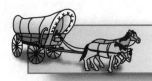

Gettysburg Address (cont.)

Bookshelf Resources

Armentrout, David and Patricia. *The Gettysburg Address*. Rourke. 2005.

Armstrong, Jennifer. *A Three-Minute Speech: Lincoln's Remarks at Gettysburg*. Aladdin Paperbacks. 2003.

Ford, Carin T. *The Battle of Gettysburg and Lincoln's Gettysburg Address*. Enslow. 2004.

Lincoln, Abraham. *The Gettysburg Address*. Houghton Mifflin. 1995.

Murphy, Jim. *The Long Road to Gettysburg*. Clarion. 1992.

Olson, Steven P. *Lincoln's Gettysburg Address: A Primary Source Investigation*. Rosen Central Primary Source. 2005.

Tanaka, Shelley. *Gettysburg: The Legendary Battle and the Address That Inspired a Nation*. Hyperion Books for Children. 2003.

Related Websites

http://www.loc.gov/exhibits/gadd/gaphot.html
("The Only Known Photograph of President Lincoln at the Dedication of the Civil War Cemetery at Gettysburg, Pennsylvania November 19, 1863," The Library of Congress)

http://www.loc.gov/exhibits/treasures/trm095.html
("Battle of Gettysburg," The Library of Congress)

http://www.gettysburg.com/bog/bogstory/story1.htm
("The Extraordinary Story of the Battle of Gettysburg," Gettysburg.com)

http://www.virtualgettysburg.com/vg/how/index.html
("See Virtual Gettysburg in Action," Another Software Miracle, LLC)

http://showcase.netins.net/web/creative/lincoln/tours/gettytour.htm
("Lincoln at Gettysburg Photo Tour," Abraham Lincoln Online)

http://www.eyewitnesstohistory.com/gtburg.htm
("The Battle of Gettysburg, 1863," Ibis Communications)

http://memory.loc.gov/cgi-bin/query/v?ammem/cwar:0185-0209:T11
("Selected Civil War Photographs, 1861–1865," The Library of Congress American Memory)

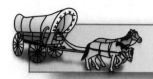

Assassination of Lincoln

RELATED THEMES: Abraham Lincoln, Civil War, Presidents, Journaling, Fictional Narrative

LITERATURE CONNECTION: Rinaldi, Ann. *An Acquaintance with Darkness.* Harcourt Brace. 1997.

Newly orphaned, fourteen-year-old Emily wants to move in with her friend, Annie Surratt. Her plans fall through when Annie's mother is locked up for taking part in the assassination of President Lincoln. Emily has to reside with her uncle, Dr. Valentine, who is involved in secret medical research.

NATIONAL STANDARDS CORRELATION

IRA/NCTE 5: Students employ a wide range of strategies as they write and use different writing process elements appropriately to communicate with different audiences for a variety of purposes.

NCSS Standard IId: (Time, Continuity, & Change) identify and use processes important to reconstructing and reinterpreting the past, such as using a variety of sources, providing, validating, and weighing evidence for claims, checking credibility of sources, and searching for causality

NHS Standard 2F: (Historical Comprehension) Appreciate historical perspectives—(a) describing the past on its own terms, through the eyes and experiences of those who were there, as revealed through their literature, diaries, letters, debates, arts, artifacts, and the like; (b) considering the historical context in which the event unfolded—the values, outlook, options, and contingencies of that time and place; and (c) avoiding "present-mindedness," judging the past solely in terms of present-day norms and values.

ACTIVITY ONE

Primary Source: http://digital.library.mcgill.ca/lincoln/exhibit/imgdisplay.php?item=3&sec=4&taft= ("Taft Journal," McGill University)

Directions: On April 14, 1865, President and Mrs. Abraham Lincoln were attending a performance at Ford's Theatre. At 10:00 p.m., the President was shot by John Wilkes Booth. He was carried unconscious to a neighboring house where Dr. C. S. Taft attended him. Dr. Taft kept a detailed record of Lincoln's injuries and care until his death. Students read Dr. Taft's journal. They research the events surrounding the assassination and death of Lincoln. From the perspective of an eyewitness, students write journal entries about the events surrounding the assassination.

ACTIVITY TWO

Primary Source: http://memory.loc.gov/ammem/alhtml/alrb/stbdsd/00801200/001.html ("Six Printed Mourning Cards," The Library of Congress American Memory)

Directions: In 1865, the nation went into mourning following the assassination of President Abraham Lincoln by John Wilkes Booth. Within days, as custom required, mourning cards were printed. Students examine President Lincoln's mourning cards, noting the different styles and layouts. After researching the life of John Wilkes Booth, they design a mourning card for him.

Assassination of Lincoln (cont.)

ACTIVITY THREE

Primary Source: http://memory.loc.gov/ammem/alhtml/alrb/stbdsd/00800800/001.html ("Ephemera Gallery: 'The Nation Mourns'," The Library of Congress American Memory)

Directions: The assassination of President Abraham Lincoln shocked a nation. Mourners showed their respect to his memory in many ways. Students examine "The Nation Mourns," a memorial poem printed as a handbill, and follow the same format to create a poem for someone they respect.

Bookshelf Resources

Burgan, Michael. *The Assassination of Abraham Lincoln*. Compass Point Books. 2005.

Freedman, Russell. *Lincoln: A Photobiography*. Clarion. 1987.

Holzer, Harold. *The President is Shot!: The Assassination of Abraham Lincoln*. Boyds Mill Press. 2004.

Otfinoski, Steven. *John Wilkes Booth and the Civil War*. Blackbirch Press. 1999.

Somerlott, Robert. *The Lincoln Assassination in American History*. Enslow. 1998.

Related Websites

http://www.law.umkc.edu/faculty/projects/ftrials/lincolnconspiracy/lincolnnews.html ("Newspaper Accounts of the Lincoln Assassination, Conspiracy Trial, and Execution of Convicted Conspirators," University of Missouri-Kansas City)

http://www.si.edu/archives/documents/deathoflincoln.htm ("Mary Henry: Eyewitness to the Civil War in the City of Washington," Smithsonian Institution)

http://memory.loc.gov/ammem/alhtml/alrgall.html ("Assassination of President Abraham Lincoln," The Library of Congress American Memory)

Transcontinental Railroad

RELATED THEMES: Chinese Americans, Immigrants, Stereotyping, Manifest Destiny, Migration, Transportation, Railroads, Letter Writing, Fictional Narrative

LITERATURE CONNECTION: Yin. *Coolies*. Philomel Books. 2001.

Shek and Wong, two brothers, emigrate from China to the United States. They are hired by the Central Pacific Railroad to build the railroad that would connect the nation.

NATIONAL STANDARDS CORRELATION

<u>IRA/NCTE 7:</u> Students conduct research on issues and interests by generating ideas and questions, and by posing problems. They gather, evaluate, and synthesize data from a variety of sources (e.g., print and nonprint texts, artifacts, people) to communicate their discoveries in ways that suit their purpose and audience.

<u>NCSS IVg:</u> (Individual Development & Identity) identify and interpret examples of stereotyping, conformity, and altruism

<u>NSH Era 6, Standard 2A:</u> The student understands the sources and experiences of the new immigrants.

ACTIVITY ONE

Primary Source: http://www.ourdocuments.gov/doc.php?flash=true&doc=47
("Chinese Exclusion Act, 1882," U.S. National Archives & Records Administration)

Directions: After the transcontinental railroad was completed, many of the Chinese labor force settled in California. They became the target of prejudicial laws and ethnic violence. Students research the events leading up to the passing of the Chinese Exclusion Act. They concentrate on the treatment of the Chinese in California. Students, pretending they are Shek and Wong, compose a letter home to their mother. In this letter, they include factual information about the atmosphere of prejudice that prevailed in California.

ACTIVITY TWO

Primary Source: http://hdl.loc.gov/loc.rbc/rbpe.08600600
("Go west over the Missouri Pacific or Atlantic & Pacific railroad, via Saint Louis [Time tables, rates, etc.] St. Louis [186-?]," The Library of Congress American Memory)

Directions: The transcontinental railroad connected the United States from East to West, allowing the nation to become a mobile society. Students examine the primary source. Students imagine they are traveling west on the train. Integrating information taken from the primary source, they design individual railroad tickets for a family of four traveling from St. Louis to a destination of their choice.

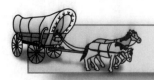

Transcontinental Railroad (cont.)

 Bookshelf Resources

Ambrose, Stephen E. *Nothing Like it in the World: The Men Who Built the Transcontinental Railroad, 1863–1869*. Simon and Schuster. 2000.

Barter, James. *Building the Transcontinental Railroad*. Lucent Books. 2002.

Burger, James P. *The Transcontinental Railroad*. PowerKids Press. 2002.

Durbin, William. *The Journal of Sean Sullivan: A Transcontinental Railroad Worker*. Scholastic. 1999.

Halpern, Monica. *Railroad Fever: Building the Transcontinental Railroad*. National Geographic. 2004.

Houghton, Gillian. *The Transcontinental Railroad: A Primary Source History of America's First Coast-to-Coast Railroad*. Rosen Central Primary Source. 2003.

Streissguth, Thomas. *The Transcontinental Railroad*. Lucent Books. 2000.

Yep, Laurence. *Dragon's Gate*. HarperCollins. 1993.

 Related Websites

http://memory.loc.gov/ammem/award99/cubhtml/cichome.html
("*The Chinese in California, 1850-1925,*" The Library of Congress American Memory)

http://www.historicaldocuments.com/ChineseExclusionActlg.htm
("Chinese Exclusion Act (1882)," Americans.net)

http://www.lib.utexas.edu/maps/historical/chinese_pop_1872.jpg
("Chinese Population Compiled From 9th Census," The University of Texas-Austin)

http://americanhistory.si.edu/onthemove/exhibition/exhibition_2_1.html
("America on the Move: Community Dreams," Smithsonian National Museum of American History Behring Center)

http://www.cprr.org/Museum/
("Central Pacific Railroad Photographic History Museum," Central Pacific Railroad)

http://www.sfmuseum.org/hist1/rail.html
("Driving the Last Spike," The Virtual Museum of the City of San Francisco)

http://www.pbs.org/wgbh/amex/tcrr/
("Transcontinental Railroad," Public Broadcasting Service)

Life on the Prairie

RELATED THEMES: Homestead Act of 1862, Manifest Destiny, Migration, Great Plains, Pioneers, Graphic Organizers, Persuasive Writing

LITERATURE CONNECTION: Turner, Ann. *Dakota Dugout*. MacMillan. 1985.

A grandmother tells her granddaughter about her adventure as a bride living in a sod house on the Dakota prairie. Her memories of snakes falling from the sod ceiling, unpredictable weather, and crops dying in the field, paint a realistic picture of homesteading.

NATIONAL STANDARDS CORRELATION

IRA/NCTE 7: Students conduct research on issues of interest by generating ideas and questions, and by posing problems. They gather, evaluate, and synthesize data from a variety of sources (e.g., print and nonprint texts, artifacts, people) to communicate their discoveries in ways that suit their purpose and audience.

NCSS IIIh: (People, Places, & Environments) examine, interpret, and analyze physical and cultural patterns and their interactions, such as land use, settlement patterns, cultural transmission of customs and ideas, and ecosystems changes

NSH Standard 2I: (Historical Comprehension) Draw upon visual, literary, and musical sources including: (a) photographs, paintings, cartoons, and architectural drawings; (b) novels, poetry, and plays; and, (c) folk, popular, and classical music, to clarify, illustrate, or elaborate upon information presented in the historical narrative.

ACTIVITY ONE
Primary Source: http://memory.loc.gov/cgi-bin/query/r?ammem/ngp:@field%28NUMBER+@band%28ndfahult+c061%29%29
("John Bakken Sod House, Milton, North Dakota," The Library of Congress American Memory)

Directions: "Sodbusters," or homesteaders, on the prairie in 1862, constructed homes of sod and grass because trees were scarce on the Great Plains. Students create a model of a sod house with written directions that explain how homesteaders built the dwelling.

ACTIVITY TWO
Primary Source: http://www.ourdocuments.gov/doc.php?flash=true&doc=31
("Homestead Act (1862)," U.S. National Archives & Records Administration)

Directions: The Homestead Act of 1862 allowed settlers to acquire 160 acres of public land. Homesteaders were required to live on the land for five years. Sod houses were common dwellings built by the settlers. Students research life in a "soddy" and list the advantages and disadvantages of living in this type of home. Using their research, students create classified ads to sell a sod house.

Life on the Prairie (cont.)

Bookshelf Resources

Armstrong, Jennifer. *Black-Eyed Susan: A Novel*. Knopf. 1997.

Bial, Raymond. *Frontier Home*. Houghton Mifflin. 1993.

Lawlor, Laurie. *Addie Across the Prairie*. Albert Whitman. 1986.

Love, D. Anne. *A Year Without Rain*. Holiday House. 2000.

MacLachlan, Patricia. *Sarah, Plain and Tall*. Harper & Row. 1985.

Rounds, Glen. *Sod Houses on the Great Plains*. Holiday House. 1995.

Turner, Ann Warren. *Grasshopper Summer*. MacMillan. 1989.

Wilder, Laura Ingalls. *By the Shores of Silver Lake*. Harper. 1953.

Wilder, Laura Ingalls. *On the Banks of Plum Creek*. Harper. 1953.

Related Websites

http://memory.loc.gov/ammem/award97/ndfahtml/ngphome.html
("Collection of 900 photographs about people living on the Northern Great Plains during the late 1800's,"
The Library of Congress American Memory)

http://www.nebraskastudies.org/0500/frameset_reset.html?http://www.nebraskastudies.org/0500/stories/0501_0101.html
("Challenges of Living on the Plains," nebraskastudies.org)

http://www.pbs.org/wnet/frontierhouse/resources/lp3.html
("Frontier House," Public Broadcasting Service)

http://www.pbs.org/wnet/frontierhouse/quiz.php
("Do You Have What it Takes to be a Pioneer?," Public Broadcasting Service)

http://pbskids.org/stantonanthony/frontier_girl.html
("A Day in the Life: History Game," Public Broadcasting Service)

Chisholm Trail

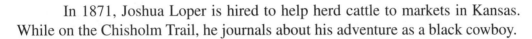

RELATED THEMES: Cowboys, Cattle Drives, Trails, Railroads, Multiple Perspectives, Letter Writing, Fictional Narrative, Poetry

LITERATURE CONNECTION: Myers, Walter Dean. *The Journal of Joshua Loper: A Black Cowboy*. Scholastic. 1999.

In 1871, Joshua Loper is hired to help herd cattle to markets in Kansas. While on the Chisholm Trail, he journals about his adventure as a black cowboy.

NATIONAL STANDARDS CORRELATION

<u>IRA/NCTE 4:</u> Students adjust their use of spoken, written, and visual language (e.g., conventions, style, vocabulary) to communicate effectively with a variety of audiences and for different purposes.

<u>NCSS IIc:</u> (Time, Continuity, & Change) identify and describe selected historical periods and patterns of change across cultures, such as the rise of civilizations, the development of transportation systems, the growth and breakdown of colonial systems, and others

<u>NSH Standard 4B:</u> (Historical Research Capabilities) Obtain historical data from a variety of sources, including: library and museum collections, historic sites, historical photos, journals, diaries, eyewitness accounts, newspapers, and the like; documentary films, oral testimony from living witnesses, censuses, tax records, city directories, statistical compilations, and economic indicators.

ACTIVITY ONE

Primary Source: http://photoswest.org/cgi-bin/imager?10021563+X-21563
("Black Cowboy and Horse," Denver Public Library Western History Photos Database)

Directions: Texas ranchers hired men for one dollar a day to drive herds to markets in Kansas. Most cowboys were young men in their teens and early twenties. Some of the cowboys were of African-American, Hispanic, or Native American descent. Dust, heat, injuries, rustlers, and stampedes forced the young men to work together as a team to survive. Students examine the primary source and research cowboy life. Using the information, they write a letter home, from the perspective of a young cowboy, about the experience of driving cattle along the Chisholm Trail.

ACTIVITY TWO

Primary Source: http://www.kshs.org/publicat/khq/1939/39_1_hull.htm
("Cowboy Ballads," Kansas State Historical Society)

Directions: A trail drive of cattle from Texas to Kansas took approximately three months. It was a hard journey for the cowboys. They spent long hours on horseback moving cattle along the hot, dusty Chisholm Trial. To relieve the boredom, they made up ballads about cowboy life on the trail. They sang these songs to settle the herd and for entertainment. Students examine the primary source, focusing on the stories told through song. They research the cowboy lifestyle and use the information to compose a ballad.

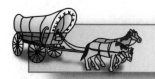

Chisholm Trail (cont.)

Bookshelf Resources

Cusic, Don. *Cowboys and the Wild West: An A–Z Guide From the Chisholm Trail to the Silver Screen.* Facts on File. 1994.

DeAngelis, Gina. *The Black Cowboys.* Chelsea House Publishers. 1997.

Freedman, Russell. *Cowboys of the Wild West.* Clarion. 1985.

Kalman, Bobbie. *Life on the Trail.* Crabtree. 1999.

Santella, Andrew. *The Chisholm Trail.* Children's Press. 1997.

Stanley, Jerry. *Cowboys & Longhorns.* Crown Publishers. 2003.

Related Websites

http://www.kancoll.org/books/mccoy/
("Historic Sketches of the Cattle Trade of the West and Southwest," The Kansas Collection)

http://www.nps.gov/grko/newtraildrives.htm
("Trail Drives," National Park Service)

http://photoswest.org/cgi-bin/imager?10021936+X-21936
("Cowboys in Camp," Denver Public Library Western History Photos Database)

http://memory.loc.gov/cgi-bin/query/r?ammem/wpa:@field(DOCID+@lit(wpa118130107))#181301070001
("Mrs. Mabel Luke Madison," The Library of Congress American Memory)

http://photoswest.org/cgi-bin/imager?00071020+MCC-1020
("Ready to Break Camp," Denver Public Library Western History Photos Database)

http://photoswest.org/cgi-bin/imager?00071022+MCC-1022
("Cowboys on the Roundup," Denver Public Library Western History Photos Database)

http://www.lib.utexas.edu/maps/atlas_texas/texas_frontier_forts.jpg
("Frontier Federal Forts and Cattle Trails," University of Texas System)

Gold Rush

RELATED THEMES: Migration, Klondike Gold Rush, Economy, Letter Writing, Fictional Narrative

LITERATURE CONNECTION: Hobbs, Will. *Jason's Gold.* Morrow Junior Books. 1999.

Jason, a fifteen-year-old boy, seeks his fortune in the Klondike gold fields. The story is filled with his adventures while traveling on the Dead Horse Trail, the Chilkoot Pass, and the Yukon River.

NATIONAL STANDARDS CORRELATION

IRA/NCTE 8: Students use a variety of technological and informational resources (e.g., libraries, databases, computer networks, video) to gather and synthesize information and to create and communicate knowledge.

NCSS IId: (Time, Continuity, & Change) identify and use processes important to reconstructing and reinterpreting the past, such as using a variety of sources, providing, validating, and weighing evidence for claims, checking credibility of sources, and searching for causality

NSH Standard 2F: (Historical Comprehension) Appreciate historical perspectives—(a) describing the past on its own terms, through the eyes and experiences of those who were there, as revealed through their literature, diaries, letters, debates, arts, artifacts, and the like; (b) considering the historical context in which the event unfolded—the values, outlook, options, and contingencies of that time and place; and (c) avoiding "present-mindedness," judging the past solely in terms of present-day norms and values.

ACTIVITY ONE

Primary Source: http://www.lib.washington.edu/specialcoll/exhibits/klondike/case4ex1.html ("Klondike Outerwear," University of Washington Libraries)

Directions: Prospectors heading north for the gold fields had to make advanced preparations and purchases. Students compile a list of outerwear that was necessary for survival in the Arctic wilderness. Based on today's prices, students calculate the current cost of the clothing list.

ACTIVITY TWO

Primary Source: http://www.library.state.ak.us/goldrush/ARCHIVES/manu1/gdust_b.htm ("The Alaska State Library Manuscripts," Alaska State Library)

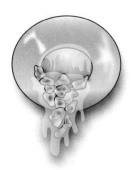

Directions: One of the popular methods for obtaining nuggets was panning for gold. Students examine the information at the above website to learn the panning technique used by miners. Simulate this activity by placing gold painted rocks of various sizes in the bottom of a child's plastic swimming pool. Cover rocks with a layer of sand and fill the pool with cold water. Using metal pie pans, students practice panning techniques.

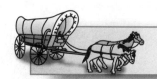

Gold Rush (cont.)

 Bookshelf Resources

Cushman, Karen. *The Ballad of Lucy Whipple*. Clarion Books, 1996.

Greenwood, Barbara. *Gold Rush Fever: A Story of the Klondike, 1898*. Kids Can Press. 2001.

Gregory, Kristiana. *Seeds of Hope: The Gold Rush Diary of Susanna Fairchild*. Scholastic. 2001.

Kay, Verla. *Gold Fever*. G. P. Putnam's. 1999.

Ketchum, Liza. *Gold Rush*. Little, Brown & Company. 1996.

Klein, James. *Gold Rush! The Young Prospector's Guide to Striking it Rich*. Tricycle Press. 1998.

London, Jack. *The Call of the Wild*. Scott, Foresman. 1959.

Van Steenwyk, Elizabeth. *The California Gold Rush*: *West With the Forty-Niners*. Franklin Watts. 1991.

Yep, Laurence. *The Journal of Wong Ming-Chung: A Chinese Miner*. Scholastic. 2000.

 Related Websites

http://www.lib.washington.edu/specialcoll/exhibits/klondike/case4ex2.html
("A Year's Supplies," University of Washington Libraries)

http://www.library.state.ak.us/goldrush/ARCHIVES/sarchive/sent_1.htm
("Letter sent by Governor recommending what to bring to Alaska. April 25,1886. 4 pages," Alaska State Library)

http://www.library.state.ak.us/goldrush/ARCHIVES/BOOKS/06.htm
("Cost for a miner's outfit. *Miners' Manual, United States, Alaska, the Klondike* by Horace Fletcher Clark, 1898," Alaska State Library)

http://www.library.state.ak.us/goldrush/ARCHIVES/npapers/97_p09.htm
("Newspaper: *Skaguay News*, December 31, 1897," Alaska State Library)

http://www.archives.gov/education/lessons/alaska/gold-rush.html
("Migration North to Alaska," U.S. National Archives & Records Administration)

Ellis Island

RELATED THEMES: Immigrants, Statue of Liberty, Fictional Narrative

LITERATURE CONNECTION: Bunting, Eve. *A Picnic in October*. Harcourt Brace. 1999.

Tony is really tired of going to Ellis Island every year to celebrate the birthday of Lady Liberty. He does not understand what the Statue of Liberty means to his grandmother. He discovers the true meaning of the statue when he encounters a woman who does not speak English.

NATIONAL STANDARDS CORRELATION

<u>IRA/NCTE 4:</u> Students adjust their use of the spoken, written, and visual language (e.g., conventions, style, vocabulary) to communicate effectively with a variety of audiences and for different purposes.

<u>NCSS Xb:</u> (Civic Ideals & Practices) identify and interpret sources and examples of the rights and responsibilities of citizens

<u>NSH Era 6, Standard 2A:</u> The student understands the sources and experiences of the new immigrants.

ACTIVITY ONE

Primary Source: http://www.jwa.org/exhibits/wov/lazarus/el9.html
("The New Colossus from Emma Lazarus' Copy Book, 1883," Jewish Women's Archives)

Directions: Many of the immigrants who came to the United States arrived jobless and penniless. They were far from their families and spoke only their native language. Immigrants made sacrifices to come to this new land. Why would they leave their homeland for America? In the poem, "New Colossus," is the phrase "yearning to breathe free." Students design a travel brochure highlighting freedoms enjoyed by the citizens of the United States.

ACTIVITY TWO

Primary Source: http://hdl.loc.gov/loc.pnp/det.4a27701
("Liberty Enlightening the World," The Library of Congress American Memory)

Directions: Arriving in New York harbor, immigrants are greeted by Lady Liberty. If they had cell phones and could call home as they entered the harbor, what would the immigrants say? Students compose a dialogue between a new immigrant and someone in his or her native country. The conversation should express the emotions felt at the sight of the Statue of Liberty.

Ellis Island (cont.)

 ## Bookshelf Resources

Auch, Mary Jane. *Ashes of Roses*. Holt. 2002.

Bierman, Carol. *Journey to Ellis Island: How My Father Came to America*. Hyperion Books for Children. 1998.

Kroll, Steven. *Ellis Island: Doorway to Freedom*. Holiday House. 1995.

Maestro, Betsy. *Coming to America: The Story of Immigration*. Scholastic. 1996.

Sandler, Martin W. *Island of Hope: The Story of Ellis Island and the Journey to America*. Scholastic. 2004.

Wepman, Dennis. *Immigration: From the Founding of Virginia to the Closing of Ellis Island*. Facts on File. 2002.

Woodruff, Elvira. *The Memory Coat*. Scholastic Press. 1999.

 ## Related Websites

http://memory.loc.gov/learn/features/immig/introduction.html
("Immigration," The Library of Congress American Memory)

http://memory.loc.gov/learn/features/immig/interv/toc.php
("Interviews with Today's Immigrants," The Library of Congress American Memory)

http://www.ellisisland.com
("Ellis Island History," Ellis Island Immigration Museum)

http://www.nps.gov/stli/prod02.htm#Statue%20of
("Statue of Liberty National Monument and Ellis Island," National Park Service)

http://www.historychannel.com/ellisisland/index2.html
("Ellis Island," A & E Television Networks)

http://www.pbs.org/wgbh/amex/goldman/peopleevents/e_ellis.html
("People & Events: Immigration and Deportation at Ellis Island," Public Broadcasting Service)

Women's Suffrage Movement

RELATED THEMES: Women's Rights, Time Line, Drama

LITERATURE CONNECTION: Lasky, Kathryn. *A Time for Courage: The Suffragette Diary of Kathleen Bowen*. Scholastic. 2002.

In 1917, while World War I is raging in Europe, the suffrage movement is being fought on the home front. Thirteen-year-old Kathleen Bowen journals her daily life in Washington, D.C., including her efforts to support the protest activities of her suffragette mother.

NATIONAL STANDARDS CORRELATION

IRA/NCTE 7: Students conduct research on issues and interests by generating ideas and questions, and by posing problems. They gather, evaluate, and synthesize data from a variety of sources (e.g., print and nonprint texts, artifacts, people) to communicate their discoveries in ways that suit their purpose and audience.

NCSS Vb: (Individuals, Groups, & Institutions) analyze group and institutional influences on people, events, and elements of culture

NSH Era 4, Standard 4C: Demonstrate understanding of changing gender roles and ideas and activities of women reformers

ACTIVITY ONE

Primary Source: http://www.ourdocuments.gov/doc.php?flash=true&doc=63&pages=transcript ("Transcript of 19th Amendment to the U.S. Constitution: Women's Right to Vote (1920)," U.S. National Archives & Records Administration)

Directions: In 1920, Congress passed the 19th Amendment to the United States Constitution. This amendment guaranteeing women the right to vote came after many decades of hard work by suffragettes. Students research the women's suffrage movement. Applying their research, they prepare a time line highlighting the major events of the movement.

ACTIVITY TWO

Primary Source: http://historymatters.gmu.edu/search.php?function=print&id=4964 ("Suffrage in Print: Alice Duer Miller's Satiric Journalism," History Matters)

Directions: Lucretia Mott, Elizabeth Cady Stanton, and Susan B. Anthony were famous leaders of the early women's suffrage movement; however, they died before seeing the passage of the 19th Amendment. The protest they began continued to be fought into the twentieth century by women like Alice Duer Miller. Miller was a columnist for the *New York Tribune*, and her satirical writings provided a nationwide platform for the cause. Students use the primary source as a script for performing a Reader's Theatre.

Women's Suffrage Movement (cont.)

 Bookshelf Resources

Adams, Colleen. *Women's Suffrage: A Primary Source History of the Women's Rights Movement in America*. Rosen Central Primary Source. 2003.

Bausum, Ann. *With Courage and Cloth: Winning the Fight for a Woman's Right to Vote*. National Geographic. 2004.

Duffy, James. *Radical Red*. Scribner's. 1993.

Fritz, Jean. *You Want Women to Vote, Lizzie Stanton?*. Putnam. 1995.

Kops, Deborah. *Women's Suffrage*. Blackbirch Press. 2004.

McCully, Emily Arnold. *The Ballot Box Battle*. Knopf. 1996.

Monroe, Judy. *The Susan B. Anthony Women's Voting Rights Trial: A Headline Court Case*. Enslow. 2002.

Nash, Carol Rust. *The Fight for Women's Right to Vote in American History*. Enslow. 1998.

 Related Websites

http://hdl.loc.gov/loc.rbc/rbpe.13200300
("Justice. Equality. Why Women Want to Vote. Women are Citizens, and Wish to do Their Civic Duty," The Library of Congress American Memory)

http://www.law.umkc.edu/faculty/projects/ftrials/anthony/sbahome.html
("The Trial of Susan B. Anthony, 1873," Famous Trials by Doug Linder)

http://hdl.loc.gov/loc.rbc/rbnawsa.n3348
("Are Women People? A Book of Rhymes for Suffrage Times by Alice Duer Miller," The Library of Congress American Memory)

http://hdl.loc.gov/loc.rbc/rbpe.16000300
("Declaration and Protest of the Women of the United States by the National Woman Suffrage Association. July 4th, 1876," The Library of Congress American Memory)

http://www.rochester.edu/SBA/history.html
("Suffrage History," The Anthony Center for Women's Leadership, University of Rochester)

http://memory.loc.gov/ammem/naw/nawshome.html
("Votes for Women: Selections From the National American Woman Suffrage Association Collection, 1848–1921," The Library of Congress American Memory)

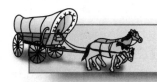

Stock Market Crash, 1929

RELATED THEMES: Great Depression, Economy, Homeless, Stereotyping, Cause and Effect, Fictional Narrative

LITERATURE CONNECTION: DeFelice, Cynthia. *Nowhere to Call Home*. Farrar Straus & Giroux. 1999.

Frances Elizabeth Barrow's father commits suicide after losing his money in the stock market crash. Frances, who is now a flat-broke, twelve-year-old orphan, decides to "ride the rails" traveling as a hobo.

NATIONAL STANDARDS CORRELATION
<u>IRA/NCTE 2:</u> Students read a wide range of literature from many periods in many genres to build an understanding of the many dimensions (e.g., philosophical, ethical, aesthetic) of human experience.
<u>NCSS IVg:</u> (Individual Development & Identity) identify and interpret examples of stereotyping, conformity, and altruism
<u>NSH Era 8, Standard 1B:</u> The student understands how American life changed during the 1930s.

ACTIVITY ONE
Primary Source: http://xroads.virginia.edu/~MA01/white/hobo/handcov.html
("*Hoboes of America*" *Incorporated 1939 Yearbook, Encyclopedia and Reference Manual, Vol. 1,*" The University of Virginia)

Directions: While reading *Nowhere to Call Home*, students generate a list of "hobo slang" words found in the story. Using the hobo dictionary section of the primary source, students write a definition for each of the slang words. They research the life of a hobo. Using the events in the story, "hobo slang," and their research, students design a game, entitled "Riding the Rails." The game should include a game board, movement cards, and rules. (Example of movement cards: "You mooch a bag of day-old doughnuts from a nice baker. Move ahead 1 space," and "A bull pulls you off the train. Go back 3 spaces.")

ACTIVITY TWO
Primary Source: http://www.nytimes.com/learning/general/onthisday/big/1029.html#article
("Stocks Collapse in 16,410,030-Share Day, But Rally at Close Cheers Brokers; Bankers Optimistic to Continue Aid," *The New York Times*)

Directions: In the 1930s, the Federal Theater Project created a new type of theater called "A Living Newspaper" with the purpose of dramatizing contemporary and historical events (see Related Websites). "A Living Newspaper" production was accomplished using a three-step process. First, initial research of the theme would be done. Second, researchers and scriptwriters would discuss their findings and brainstorm possible topics for expanding their research. Third, the scriptwriters would write the script by blending facts with drama. Working in teams, students follow this "three-step process" in the production of their own "Living Newspaper" on the theme of the Stock Market Crash of 1929 and its effect on the nation.

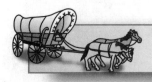

Stock Market Crash, 1929 (cont.)

Bookshelf Resources

Cummings, Priscilla. *Saving Grace*. Dutton's Children's Books. 2003.

Hadeley, Dennis. *The Amazing Thinking Machine*. Dial Books. 2002.

Ruth, Amy. *Growing Up in the Great Depression, 1929 to 1941*. Lerner Publications. 2003.

Uys, Errol Lincoln. *Riding the Rails: Teenagers on the Move During the Great Depression*. Routledge. 2003.

Woolf, Alex. *The Wall Street Crash, October 29, 1929*. Raintree Steck-Vaughn. 2003.

Wormser, Richard L. *Growing Up in the Great Depression*. Atheneum. 1994.

Wroble, Lisa A. *Kids During the Great Depression*. Powerkids Press. 1999.

Related Websites

http://xroads.virginia.edu/%7EMA04/mccain/play/intro.htm
("A Living Newspaper," The University of Virginia)

http://newdeal.feri.org/sevier/essays/gdess.htm
("Always Lend a Helping Hand: Sevier County Remembers the Great Depression," New Deal Network)

http://www.farmers.com/FarmComm/AmericanPromise/downloadables/homelessness/home_ex10.html
("Boy and Girl Tramps," Farmers' Insurance)

http://www.english.uiuc.edu/maps/depression/photoessay.htm
("Photo Essay on the Great Depression," University of Illinois at Champaign-Urbana)

http://historymatters.gmu.edu/d/25
("The Bum as Con Artist: An Undercover Account of the Great Depression," History Matters)

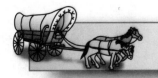

Dust Bowl

RELATED THEMES: Great Depression, Soil Conservation, Migration, Farming, Explanatory Writing

LITERATURE CONNECTION: Raven, Margot Theis. *Angels in the Dust.* BridgeWater Books. 1997.

     Annie and her family live on a farm in Oklahoma during the Dust Bowl years. They face many hardships. Her mother dies of "dust pneumonia," their crops wither in the fields, and their home burns.

NATIONAL STANDARDS CORRELATION

IRA/NCTE 8: Students use a variety of technological and informational resources (e.g., libraries, databases, computer networks, video) to gather and synthesize information and to create and communicate knowledge.

NCSS IIIj: (People, Places, & Environments) observe and speculate about social and economic effects of environmental changes and crises resulting from phenomena such as floods, storms, and drought

NSH Era 8, Standard 1B: The student understands how American life changed during the 1930s.

ACTIVITY ONE

Primary Source: http://www.fdrlibrary.marist.edu/images/photodb/27-0723a.gif
("Dust Storm, Rolla, Kansas," The Franklin D. Roosevelt Presidential Library and Museum)

Directions: In the 1930s, rolling dust storms swept across the Great Plains with devastating effects on the people and land. Many people developed a fatal respiratory problem called "dust pneumonia." After examining the photograph of the dust storm approaching Rolla, Kansas, students research Dust Bowl storms. Working in teams, students create informational pamphlets identifying the effects of a dust storm on public health and the proper emergency procedures citizens should follow.

ACTIVITY TWO

Primary Source: http://xroads.virginia.edu/%7E1930s/FILM/lorentz/plow.html
("*The Plow That Broke the Plains*," The University of Virginia)

Directions: In the 1930s, drought, combined with prior mistreatment of the land, led to one of the greatest natural disasters in the United States. In 1936, the WPA sponsored the documentary, *The Plow That Broke the Plains*. This short film used verse and music to dramatize the causes that led to the Dust Bowl. Students design a multimedia presentation using the *The Plow That Broke the Plains* script (see Related Websites).

Dust Bowl (cont.)

Bookshelf Resources

Coombs, Karen Mueller. *Children of the Dust Days*. Carolrhoda Books. 2000.

Cooper, Michael L. *Dust to Eat: Drought and Depression in the 1930's*. Clarion. 2004.

De Angelis, Therese. *The Dust Bowl*. Chelsea House. 2002.

Hesse, Karen. *Out of the Dust*. Scholastic. 1997.

Janke, Katelan. *Survival in the Storm: The Dust Bowl Diary of Grace Edwards*. Scholastic. 2002.

McArthur, Debra. *The Dust Bowl and the Depression in American History*. Enslow. 2002.

Meltzer, Milton. *Driven From the Land: The Story of the Dust Bowl*. Benchmark Books. 2000.

Porter, Tracey. *Treasures in the Dust*. HarperCollins. 1997.

Yancey, Diane. *Life During the Dust Bowl*. Lucent. 2004.

Related Websites

http://xroads.virginia.edu/%7E1930s/FILM/lorentz/plowscript.html
("The Script of *The Plow That Broke the Plains*," The University of Virginia)

http://www.weru.ksu.edu/new_weru/multimedia/multimedia.html
("Wind Erosion Multimedia Archive," Kansas State University)

http://www.livinghistoryfarm.org/farminginthe30s/water–14.html
("Farming in the 1930s," Living History Farms)

http://www.nacdnet.org/outreach/awards/poster.htm
("2005 National Conservation Poster Contest," National Association of Conservation Districts)

http://www.pbs.org/wgbh/amex/dustbowl/index.html
("Surviving the Dust Bowl," WGBH Educational Foundations)

http://memory.loc.gov/ammem/afctshtml/tshome.html
("Voices From the Dust Bowl," The Library of Congress American Memory)

New Deal

RELATED THEMES: Great Depression, Economy, Franklin D. Roosevelt, Eleanor Roosevelt, Presidents, Letter Writing, Explanatory Writing, Fictional Narrative

LITERATURE CONNECTION: Skolsky, Mindy Warshaw. *Love from Your Friend, Hannah: A Novel.* DK Publishing. 1998.

The year is 1937, and Hannah is living in Grand View, New York. Hannah and Aggie, best friends, promise to write to each other after Aggie moves. Hannah keeps the promise, but Aggie doesn't respond. Hannah begins to write to other pen pals, including the President and Mrs. Roosevelt.

August, 1933

Dear Mrs. Roosevelt,
I would like to thank
you and the President
for the good work you
are doing during this
very trying time.

NATIONAL STANDARDS CORRELATION

IRA/NCTE 2: Students read a wide range of literature from many periods in many genres to build an understanding of the many dimensions (e.g., philosophical, ethical, aesthetic) of human experience.
NCSS VIc: (Power, Authority, & Governance) analyze and explain ideas and governmental mechanisms to meet needs and wants of citizens, regulate territory, manage conflict, and establish order and security
NSH Era 8, Standard 2A: The student understands the New Deal and the presidency of Franklin D. Roosevelt.

ACTIVITY ONE

Primary Source: http://newdeal.feri.org/eleanor/1h1136.htm
("Dear Mrs. Roosevelt," The New Deal Network)

Directions: During the first term of FDR's presidency, Mrs. Roosevelt received many letters from adults and children. She was unable to respond to letters individually. Mrs. Roosevelt did support New Deal programs that brought relief to young people. Two of these programs were the National Youth Administration and lunch programs in schools. Students research one of the New Deal programs that directly benefited youth. They read examples, located in the primary source, of letters Mrs. Roosevelt received from children. Students select one of the letters and write a paragraph explaining how a New Deal program could help solve the problem described in the letter.

ACTIVITY TWO

Primary Source: http://newdeal.feri.org/er/er01.htm
("Selected Writings of Eleanor Roosevelt," The New Deal Network)

Directions: In the August 1933 issue of *Woman's Home Companion,* Mrs. Roosevelt wrote, "We all know that we have less money to spend on recreation than we have had for a great many years. How can we make that money cover the needs of a real holiday? I should like to have those of you who have taken holidays inexpensively tell me what you have done." Students recall an economical vacation or trip they enjoyed. Students write letters to Mrs. Roosevelt telling her what they did on their trip.

New Deal (Cont.)

Bookshelf Resources

Burch, Robert. *Ida Early Comes Over the Mountain*. Viking Press. 1980.

Cohen, Robert, ed. *Dear Mrs. Roosevelt: Letters from Children of the Great Depression*. University of North Carolina Press. 2002.

Cooney, Barbara. *Eleanor*. Viking Press. 1996.

De Young, C. Coco. *A Letter to Mrs. Roosevelt*. Delacorte Press. 1999.

Freedman, Russell. *Eleanor Roosevelt: A Life of Discovery*. Clarion Books. 1993.

Reiman, Richard A. *The New Deal and American Youth: Ideas and Ideals in a Depression Decade*. University of Georgia Press. 1992.

Whitmore, Arvella. *The Bread Winner*. Houghton Mifflin. 1990.

Related Websites

http://newdeal.feri.org/eleanor/mymail.htm
("Dear Mrs. Roosevelt: My Mail," The New Deal Network)

http://www.authentichistory.com/audio/1930s/history/19330312_FDR_On_The_Bank_Crisis-1st_Fireside_Chat.html
("President Franklin D. Roosevelt, First Fireside Chat, on the Bank Crisis, March 12, 1933," The Authentic History Center)

http://www.whitehouse.gov/history/firstladies/ar32.html
("Anna Eleanor Roosevelt," The White House)

http://www.fdrlibrary.marist.edu/fdrbio.html
("Franklin D. Roosevelt," Franklin D. Roosevelt Presidential Library and Museum)

http://www.fdrlibrary.marist.edu/firesi90.html
("Fireside Chats of Franklin D. Roosevelt," Franklin D. Roosevelt Presidential Library and Museum)

http://www.gwu.edu/~erpapers/documents/
("The Eleanor Roosevelt Papers: The Human Rights Years, 1945–1962," George Washington University)

Bombing of Pearl Harbor

RELATED THEMES: World War II, Franklin D. Roosevelt, Presidents, Oral History, Compare and Contrast, Multiple Perspectives

LITERATURE CONNECTION: Salisbury, Graham. *Under the Blood-Red Sun*. Delacorte Press. 1994.

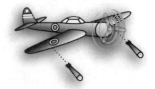

Day-to-day life seemed very ordinary for young Tomikazu Nakaji until December 7, 1941. The bombing of Pearl Harbor throws the Japanese-American community into turmoil as they are forced into relocation camps.

NATIONAL STANDARDS CORRELATION

<u>IRA/NCTE 7:</u> Students conduct research on issues and interests by generating ideas and questions and by posing problems. They gather, evaluate, and synthesize data from a variety of sources (e.g., print and nonprint texts, artifacts, people) to communicate their discoveries in ways that suit their purpose and audience.

<u>NCSS Ia:</u> (Culture) compare similarities and differences in ways groups, societies, and cultures meet human needs and concerns

<u>NSH Standard 3B:</u> (Historical Analysis and Interpretation) Consider multiple perspectives of various peoples in the past by demonstrating their differing motives, beliefs, interests, hopes, and fears.

ACTIVITY ONE

Primary Source: http://www.umkc.edu/lib/spec-col/ww2/PearlHarbor/fdr-speech.htm#doi ("Pearl Harbor—FDR's Day of Infamy Speech," University of Missouri-Kansas City Libraries)

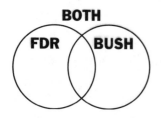

Directions: On December 8, 1941, President Franklin D. Roosevelt delivered his famous "Day of Infamy" speech to a joint session of Congress. His words united a nation against a common enemy. President George W. Bush gave a similar speech to the nation on September 11, 2001 (see Related Websites). Students compare and contrast these two speeches using a Venn diagram.

ACTIVITY TWO

Primary Source: http://www.loc.gov/folklife/vets/stories/onthebeach.html ("Experiencing War: Stories from the Veterans History Project." The Library of Congress)

Directions: The bombing of Pearl Harbor changed the lives of people in the United States. From war bonds to rationing, everyone was involved in the war effort. Oral histories have been used to record reminiscences of people who lived during World War II. The sharing of a personal experience often reveals the drama and emotions behind the event. Students listen to the oral histories, focusing on interview techniques. Using these techniques, they interview an adult about a notable event.

Bombing of Pearl Harbor (cont.)

Bookshelf Resources

Allen, Thomas B. *Remember Pearl Harbor: American and Japanese Survivors Tell Their Stories*. National Geographic Society. 2001.

Fremon, David K. *Japanese-American Internment in American History*. Enslow. 1996.

Hahn, Mary Downing. *Stepping on the Cracks*. Clarion. 1991.

Krull, Kathleen. *V is for Victory: America Remembers World War II*. Knopf. 1995.

Marx, Trish. *Echoes of World War Two*. Lerner. 1994.

Nicholson, Dorinda. *Pearl Harbor Child: A Child's View of Pearl Harbor—From Attack to Peace*. Woodson House. 2001.

Stein, R. Conrad. *"World War II in the Pacific: Remember Pearl Harbor."* Enslow. 1994.

Whitman, Sylvia. *V is for Victory: The American Home Front During World War II*. Lerner. 1993.

Related Websites

http://www.whitehouse.gov/news/releases/2001/09/20010911-16.html
("Statement by the President in His Address to the Nation, September 11, 2001," The White House)

http://parentseyes.arizona.edu/wracamps/index.html
("War Relocation Authority Camps in Arizona, 1942-1946," Through Our Parents' Eyes)

http://www.law.ou.edu/hist/japwar.html
("Congressional Declaration of War on Japan," The University of Oklahoma Law Center)

http://www.yale.edu/lawweb/avalon/wwii/p2.htm
("Message from the President to the Emperor of Japan December 6," The Avalon Project)

http://soundportraits.org/on-air/the_day_after_pearl_harbor/
("The Day after Pearl Harbor," Sound Portraits Productions)

Civil Rights

RELATED THEMES: Martin Luther King, Jr., Civil Rights Act of 1964, John F. Kennedy, Presidents, Black History Month, Public Speaking, Time Line

LITERATURE CONNECTION: Curtis, Christopher Paul. *Watsons Go to Birmingham—1963.* Delacorte Press. 1995.

In 1963, everyday life in Michigan for Byron Watson and his African-American family is uneventful. Everything changes when they must go to visit Grandma in Alabama, where prejudices are strong, and history is in the making.

NATIONAL STANDARDS CORRELATION

<u>IRA/NCTE 4:</u> Students adjust their use of spoken, written, and visual language (e.g., conventions, style, vocabulary) to communicate effectively with a variety of audiences and for different purposes.

<u>NCSS Ve:</u> (Individuals, Groups, & Institutions) identify and describe examples of tensions between belief systems and government policies and laws

<u>NSH Era 9, Standard 4A:</u> The student understands "Second Reconstruction" and its advancement of civil rights.

ACTIVITY ONE

Primary Source: http://usinfo.state.gov/usa/infousa/laws/majorlaw/civilr19.htm
("Civil Rights Act of 1964," International Information Programs)

Directions: Before 1964, life in the United States did not provide equal opportunities for all citizens. The purpose of the Civil Rights Act of 1964 was to eliminate segregation, prejudice, and inequality. One minority affected by this act was African-Americans. Students research achievements made by African-Americans since the passage of this act. Using their research, students create a time line of these accomplishments.

ACTIVITY TWO

Primary Source: http://www.mecca.org/~crights/dream.html
("I Have a Dream by Martin Luther King, Jr.," Memphis Educational Computer Connectivity Alliance)

Directions: In his speech, Dr. Martin Luther King, Jr., spoke about his vision for the nation. Four decades later, the United States is still striving to fulfill his dreams of equality for all people. Students research contemporary civil rights problems. Each student chooses an issue and composes a one- to two-minute news script. Students deliver their scripts using a nightly news format.

Civil Rights (cont.)

 ## Bookshelf Resources

Dunn, John M. *The Civil Rights Movement*. Lucent. 1998.

Finlayson, Reggie. *We Shall Overcome: The History of the American Civil Rights Movement*. Lerner. 2003.

Kelley, Robin. *Into the Fire: African Americans Since 1970*. Oxford University Press. 1996.

King, Casey and Linda Barrett Osborne. *Oh, Freedom!: Kids Talk About the Civil Rights Movement With the People Who Made it Happen*. Alfred A. Knopf. 1997.

King, Martin Luther, Jr. *I Have A Dream*. Scholastic. 1997.

McWhorter, Diane. *A Dream of Freedom: The Civil Rights Movement From 1954 to 1968*. Scholastic. 2004.

Patterson, Charles. *The Civil Rights Movement*. Facts on File. 1995.

Taylor, Kimberly Hayes. *Black Civil Rights Champions*. Oliver Press. 1995.

Woodson, Jacqueline. *The Other Side*. Putnam. 2001.

 ## Related Websites

http://www.stanford.edu/group/King/mlkpapers/
("The Martin Luther King, Jr. Papers Project," Stanford University)

http://www.thekingcenter.org/
("The Beloved Community," The King Center)

http://www.usccr.gov/
("U.S. Commission on Civil Rights," U.S. Commission on Civil Rights)

http://www.besthistorysites.net/USHistory_CivilRights.shtml
("Civil Rights," Best of History Websites)

http://nobelprize.org/peace/laureates/1964/king-bio.html
("Martin Luther King—Biography," The Nobel Foundation)

http://www.cr.nps.gov/nr/travel/civilrights/intro1.htm
("We Shall Overcome: Historic Places of the Civil Rights Movement," National Park Service)

http://tstrong.com/mlking/index.html
("Dr. Martin Luther King, Jr., Scavenger Hunt," Teresa Strong)

Index by Theme

Index by Theme (cont.)